IS **MILTON**

BETTER THAN **SHAKESPEARE?**

IS **MILTON**
BETTER THAN **SHAKESPEARE?**

NIGEL SMITH

HARVARD UNIVERSITY PRESS

CAMBRIDGE, MASSACHUSETTS

2008

LIBRARY OF CONGRESS CATALOGING-IN-PUBLICATION DATA

Smith, Nigel, 1958–

    Is Milton better than Shakespeare? / Nigel Smith.

       p.   cm.

    Includes bibliographical references and index.

    ISBN-13: 978-0-674-02832-6 (alk. paper)

    1. Milton, John, 1608–1674—Criticism and interpretation.   I. Title.

    PR3588.S556 2008

    821'.4—dc22

    2007039202

CONTENTS

BIOGRAPHICAL OUTLINE

1608   9 December. Born to John Milton and his wife, Sara, at The Spreadeagle, Bread St., London.

1615   24 November. Brother, Christopher, born.

1620   Enters St. Paul's School, under Alexander Gill. Also tutored at home, possibly earlier, by Thomas Young.

1625   12 February. Admitted to Christ's College, Cambridge, under William Chappell.

27 March. James I dies; Charles I accedes to English throne.

November? Writes epigrams on the Gunpowder Plot.

1626   Possibly temporarily suspended from college. Returns to Cambridge under Nathaniel Tovey.

1627   11 June. Lends his future father-in-law, Richard Powell, £500.

1629   26 March. Receives bachelor of arts degree.

1632   "On Shakespeare" is published.

3 July. Receives master's degree.

Retires to family home at Hammersmith to study.

1634 29 September. *Comus* is performed during the installation of Thomas Egerton, the Lord President of Wales, at Ludlow Castle.

1637 Moves with parents to Horton, Buckinghamshire.

Comus is published.

3 April. Mother dies.

10 August. Edward King drowns.

September. Considers entering Inns of Court.

1638 *Lycidas* is published in the memorial volume for Edward King, *Justa Edwardo King Naufrago*.

May. Begins tour of western Europe, passing through France, then Florence, Siena, Lucca, Rome, Bologna, Ferrara, Verona, Venice, Milan, and Naples, and returning by way of Geneva.

27 August. Charles Diodati is buried.

1639 Charles I invades Scotland.

July. Returns home.

1640 Moves to St. Bride's Churchyard. Begins to teach nephews, Edward and John Phillips, and some aristocratic children.

The Long Parliament is convened.

? "Epitaphium Damonis" is published.

30 June. Takes Richard Powell's lands in Wheatley for nonpayment of debt.

1641 May. *Of Reformation* is published.

June? *Of Prelatical Episcopacy* is published.

July. *Animadversions* is published.

1642   February. *The Reason of Church Government* is published.

May. *Apology against a Pamphlet* ["against Smectymnuus"] is published. Marries Mary Powell.

July? Mary Powell returns to her family home near Oxford.

August. The civil war begins.

October. Christopher Milton enlists with Royalists at Reading.

23 October. Battle of Edgehill takes place.

1643   1 August. *The Doctrine and Discipline of Divorce* is published.

1644   2 February. Second edition of *Doctrine and Discipline* is published.

5 June. *Of Education* is published.

2 July. Battle of Marston Moor takes place.

6 August. *The Judgement of Martin Bucer Concerning Divorce* is published.

23 November. *Areopagitica* is published.

28 December. Summoned before House of Lords.

1645   4 March. *Tetrachordon* and *Colasterion* are published.

September? Moves to larger house at Barbican.

6 October. *Poems of Mr. John Milton, Both English and Latin . . . 1645* is registered for publication.

Makes plans to marry the daughter of a Dr. Davis. Mary Powell returns.

14 June. Battle of Naseby takes place.

1646   2 January. *Poems . . . 1645* is published.

29 July. Daughter Anne is born.

1647   March. Father dies.

21 April. Moves to a smaller house in High Holborn, near Lincoln's Inn Fields.

1648   25 October. Daughter Mary is born.

1649   30 January. Charles I is executed.

13 February. *The Tenure of Kings and Magistrates* is published.

March. Invited to become secretary for the foreign tongues by Council of State. 15 March, appointed secretary at £288 per year; ordered to answer *Eikon Basilike*.

11 May. Salmasius's *Defensio Regia* appears.

16 May. *Observations on the Articles of Peace* is published.

6 October. *Eikonoklastes* is published.

19 November. Given lodgings for official work in Scotland Yard.

1650   Ordered by Council of State to answer Salmasius.

1651   24 February. *Pro Populo Anglicano Defensio* is published.

16 March. Son, John, is born.

Milton family moves to a house in Petty France, Westminster.

1652   February. Becomes totally blind toward the end of the month.

2 May. Daughter Deborah is born.

5 May. Wife, Mary, dies, probably from complications following childbirth.

16 June? Son, John, dies.

August. Following several earlier attacks on the *Defensio,* including Filmer's, Pierre du Moulin's *Regii Sanguinis Clamor* is published, in reply to Milton's *Defensio;* Milton is ordered to reply by the Council of State.

1653   20 February. Writes a letter recommending that Andrew Marvell become his assistant.

3 September. Salmasius dies.

1654   30 May. *Pro Populo Anglicano Defensio Secunda* is published.

1655   Allowed to use amanuensis to take dictation in his capacity as secretary. Resumes private scholarship, prepares Latin dictionary and Greek lexicon; possibly works on *De Doctrina Christiana* and *Paradise Lost.* Salary reduced from £288 to £150 but made a pension for life.

8 August. *Defensio Pro Se* is published.

1656   12 November. Marries Katherine Woodcock.

1657   19 October. Daughter Katherine is born.

1658   3 February. Wife, Katherine, dies.

17 March. Daughter Katherine dies.

May? Edits and publishes manuscript of Sir Walter Raleigh's *Cabinet Council.*

3 September. Oliver Cromwell dies.

1659   16 February? *A Treatise of Civil Power* is published.

22 April. Richard Cromwell dissolves Parliament.

7 May. Republic is restored.

August. *Considerations Touching the Likeliest Means to Remove Hirelings Out of the Church* is published.

20 October. Writes *Letter to a Friend, Concerning the Ruptures of the Commonwealth* (not published until 1698).

1660   23–29 February. *The Readie & Easie Way to Establish a Free Commonwealth* is published.

April. *Brief Notes upon a Sermon* is published.

May. Goes into hiding to avoid retaliation for supporting regicide.

Second edition of *The Readie & Easie Way* published.

29 May. Charles II accedes to throne.

16 June. Parliament looks into the possibility of having Milton arrested.

27 August. *Pro Populo Anglicano Defensio* and *Eikonoklastes* are publicly burned.

29 August. Milton is not excluded from Act of Indemnity.

September? Takes a house in Holborn, near Red Lion Fields; soon moves again, to Jewin St.

October? Arrested and imprisoned.

15 December. Released by order of Parliament.

17 December. Marvell protests in Parliament about the exorbitance of Milton's jail fees (£150).

1662   Begins tutoring Thomas Ellwood.

19 May. Act of Uniformity is passed.

June? Sonnet to Sir Henry Vane is published.

14 June. Vane is executed.

1663   24 February. Marries Elizabeth Minshull. Moves from Jewin Street to "a House in the artillery-walk leading to Bunhill Fields." On bad terms with his daughters; new wife allegedly had the two eldest daughters apprenticed as lacemakers.

1665   Ellwood secures a house for Milton in Chalfont St. Giles, Buckinghamshire, to escape from the plague in London.

1667	August? *Paradise Lost* is published, in ten books.
1668	*Paradise Lost* is reissued with a new title page, the arguments, and other preliminary matter.
1669	June. *Accidence Commenced Grammar* is published.
1670	*History of Britain* is published
1671	*Paradise Regained* and *Samson Agonistes* are published together.
1672	May? *Art of Logic* is published.
1673	May? *Of True Religion* is published.
	November. *Poems, &c. upon Several Occasions . . . 1673* is published.
1674	L'Estrange refuses publication license for Milton's letters of state.
	May. *Epistolae Familiares* and *Prolusiones* are published.
	2 July? Second edition of *Paradise Lost* is published, in twelve books.
	8–10 November. Dies in Bunhill house.
	12 November. Buried in St. Giles, Cripplegate.

PREFACE

This book is a provocation to as general a public as possible to reconsider the writings of John Milton. This statement is made in the year of his four hundredth birthday. I am not suggesting that it makes sense to argue that Milton is better than Shakespeare in any absolute way, but I do maintain that there are certain ways in which Milton is more salient and important than Shakespeare because he is the poet who places liberty at the center of his vision. Historically he has been more influential than Shakespeare in this respect. Milton's presence may be discerned in the formation of much of the English-speaking world's understanding of how the individual belongs to the world and how a just society should be ordered. He considers the nature or even necessity of rebellion, the need to overcome the deadening hold of custom, and the belief that liberty comes through the confrontation of contrary experiences and contrariness itself. For a great poet to address these vital public and personal themes, from sexuality and marriage to free speech, and to make them part of an astonishingly exciting, innovative, visionary literary practice, one that is explicitly dedicated to positive transformation in all spheres of human activity, is what seems to me to put Milton out in front.

My own experience with Milton, first as student and then as teacher, has incurred many debts: to all of the authors and studies mentioned in my text, and to a great many more. I am deeply and personally indebted to several colleagues for many insightful discussions concerning Milton during the last twenty-five years, in Oxford and Great Britain and in Princeton and the United States: John Carey, Bill Readings[†], Jeremy Maule[†], John Hoyles, Arthur Pollard[†], Tom Corns, David Norbrook, Sharon Achinstein, Martin Dzelzainis, Nicholas von Maltzahn, Blair Worden, John Creaser, Nicholas McDowell, Margaret Kean, Will Poole, Robert Wilcher, Annabel Patterson, Barbara Lewalski, Victoria Kahn, Stella Revard, David Loewenstein, Marshall Grossman, Jason Rosenblatt, James G. Turner, Ann Coiro, Earl Miner[†], Joanna Picciotto, Oliver Arnold, Joseph Wittreich, Stuart Curran, Stephen Fallon, Laura Knoppers, John Leonard, Gordon Teskey, and Tom Luxon. I wish there were space to thank the entire multitude of students, graduate and undergraduate, I have had the privilege to teach for their memorable work. Suffice it to say that Vincent Smithers, Warwick Thompson, Kate Thomas, Joanna Friedman, and Samuel Fallon each had a specific impact on some of the ideas I develop here. I should like to thank warmly Lindsay Waters and Phoebe Kossman at Harvard University Press for their help with this project, and Liz Duvall of Technologies 'N Typography for assiduous and expedient copyediting. For help with popular culture I am grateful to Alice Eardley, and with the art of poetry, Paul Muldoon and Jane Griffiths. Responsibility for the views and information set out in this study remains mine.

TEXTUAL NOTE

Unless otherwise stated, quotations from Milton's poetry are taken from John Milton, *Complete Shorter Poems,* ed. John Carey, 2d ed. (Longman, 1997) (*CSP*), and John Milton, *Paradise Lost,* ed. Alastair Fowler, 2d ed. (Longman, 1998). Quotations from the prose are based on John Milton, *Complete Prose Works,* ed. Don M. Wolfe, 8 vols. (Yale University Press, 1953–1982) (*CPW*), which is faithful to the early published editions. As with the Longman poetry editions, I have kept the punctuation but modernized the spelling.

IS **MILTON**

BETTER THAN **SHAKESPEARE?**

As I begin to write this book, the planet on which I live and work is transfixed by an international predicament that is intimately related to my subject. A nation-state with very considerable resources of nature, human wit, and technology has become the most powerful state in the world: the United States of America. It has done so in part through a theory of liberty that owes not a little to the author whose writings I'll be examining. Being so powerful, it has inherited the role of world policeman, and as such finds itself on the receiving end of a deadly campaign by those whose conflicting ideals, having been failed by every nation-state, can be pursued only through another kind of opposition. I'm talking, of course, about the terrorists of Al-Qaeda.

Islamic terrorists do not care for Western liberalism, so they say, believing only in a very strict interpretation of the Koran and all of the denial that comes with it: of gender, sexuality, education, public consciousness, and so on. Indeed, Islamic fundamentalism often looks today like the kind of violent bigotry that was associated with so many of Milton's coreligionists, the Puritans. The tightening of public controls—visible at airports and train stations—and the considerably enhanced powers of police investigation and detention that Western governments have adopted in order to combat the threat of terrorism are frequently denounced as a fatal compromise of the very principles of liberty on which our cherished open society is based. Islamic fundamentalists accuse America and its allies of perpetrating acts of imperialist aggression by backing Israel and corrupt, authoritarian Arab regimes. These nations display, it is alleged, a quest for control of the world's oil resources as a thinly disguised ulterior motive. Traditionally, liberty-loving republicans do not approve of imperialism: "We are not a conquering people," said President Bush at the beginning of the American and British invasion of Iraq. The defeat of terrorism, as it has been strategized thus far, involves the compromise of Western liberty (to a degree that makes some Christian fundamentalist supporters of President Bush, the descendents of the seventeenth-century Puritans, happy) in a cause that appears to many modern Western defenders of liberty as imperialistic and unjust. It is a knotty, paradoxical, bloody, unjust, depressing, disgraceful, unconscionable mess.

Or take the longer view. The Western powers evolved from early modern nation-states, most of which rose to a degree of world influence by creating mercantile and then political empires in other parts of the globe. Britain was the dominant world power in the nineteenth century, the United States for much of the twentieth, especially the last quarter. The West consists of liberal democracies that have relatively well educated middle classes and permit comparatively large degrees of personal autonomy—the ability of individuals to believe as they wish and to accumulate large sums of personal wealth. And the West has been pitted in a cold war against communist powers while seeking to maintain preeminent economic, political, and cultural influence in other parts of the world. Without the "dictatorship of the proletariat" to contend with after the collapse of communism in the late 1980s, the United States looks hypocritical to those elsewhere, using democracy as a mask for Western exploitation.

Yet we might say that the upside of this predicament is the worldwide spread of computer-driven information technology, enabling communication on a scale and at a rate that would have left the inventors of the printed book gaping in awe. Many people in the world now enjoy a "democracy of communication" unimaginable decades ago, a popular access to information and the power of communication that has aided not only learning and commerce but also political activity and indeed even terrorism. Will the microchip revolution be the savior of the planet, as we all battle the sustained and intensifying effects of heavy industry and face ecological catastrophe?

John Milton's career and writings are vitally part of these very contemporary perspectives, even though he lived more than three hundred years ago. This is largely because Milton's writings played such a dominant role in the discussions and definitions of liberty that surrounded the founding of the United States, connecting political theory and theology to widely read poetic literature.[1] Most of the founding fathers read Milton and revered him. When Americans hear Milton read aloud, they hear the American constitution, because it is Milton's prose that echoes originally in the voices of Adams and Jefferson. From then through Emerson and down to our own day, Milton and his writings have been placed, one way or another, at the center of what is meant to be quintessentially American. The Liberty Fund, a "private, educational foundation established to encourage the study of the ideal of a society of free and responsible individuals," devotes a sizable part of its website to Milton's poetry and prose and a discussion of his work. Milton's voice has been equally admired and reviled by his countrymen, the English, who adore him as a poet but have remained largely hostile to his defamation of monarchy, even to the extent of converting him into a national poet by forgetting the partisan fissures that run through his works. But Western liberty of all kinds agrees that contemplative reading of serious issues is a proper end in itself, and Milton's theorizing of the liberty to read as one of the highest goals of civilization is generally revered. Al-Qaeda would have all books except the Koran abolished. Milton's writings are indelibly part of our civilization and its values, be they old-fashioned liberal humanist ones or market-driven monetarism, and generations of educated people have testified to the hold of his works, especially, of course, his magnificent epic poem *Paradise Lost*.

This book is a study not merely of why Milton continues to be relevant but of how he is still of use to us in our current predicaments, and of how he is more thoughtfully progressive and an even better poet for these reasons than we ever realized.

To use Milton to think through our contemporary dilemmas means to go back to appreciate the nature of his achievement. In summary form, that achievement sounds stupendous. He set out from an early age to become the complete poet: to master the art of poetry and then to write the greatest heroic poem in his own language, in a conscious dialogue with the best precepts of poetry and poetic achievement in ancient and more recent European languages. While he did this, programmatically and determinedly, it was also an interrupted process, and along the way he theorized religious, political, and civil liberty, including divorce and a theology of free will. He analyzed the nature of tyranny, he explored the ways in which republican liberty might be known to English people, and he defended the English republic to a European readership. He experimented with imagining different kinds of constitutional republicanism and debated with famous contemporaries, such as Harrington and Hobbes, the best way to form and run a state. He was in a good position to do so, because from 1649 until 1659–1660 he was a senior civil servant for both non-monarchical governments, the republic and the Protectorate. He was in charge of correspondence with foreign regimes, and before that he had some responsibility for licensing books. He was involved in state-funded attempts to generate a new republican culture of letters. His prose writings themselves are a kind of poetry, in which the vision of liberty is elaborated. Implicit within them are patterns of thinking and writing in a state of liberty, and as I shall show, they are of great value to us. All of these fine achievements were then recast during his later years (when he lived in modest retirement, officially shunned for his Puritanism and republicanism) in his three great poetic works, *Paradise Lost, Paradise Regained,* and *Samson Agonistes,* albeit more pessimistically, but no less thoughtfully, and in many ways more so. Soon after its publication, *Paradise Lost* was recognized as the greatest poem in the language, despite the repugnance for Milton's political and religious views felt by some of his most eminent admirers. The admiration for the poem in Britain led to the construction of Milton's reputation as the preeminent national poet, a reputation for the most part at odds with Milton's views of English national achievements and with contemporary views of his republicanism.

The Milton I present may best be described as *libertine,* in the sense of a poet who dares to speculate on the highest and most perplexing matters in the most challenging of literary ways. He remade

English literature, but in doing so he advanced a series of courageous heretical views that went clean against the dominant moral, religious, and political orthodoxies of his time. The majesty of his writing embodies that sense of rebellion, even as it honestly admits to the energy required by such a struggle against custom and the contradictions that such an enterprise necessarily involves. Even now, I believe that the nature and complexity of that contradictory energy is not appreciated, even by Milton specialists, and it is largely my purpose to set that record straight. In this way, the reach of Milton's achievements is far greater than Shakespeare's. However much we celebrate Shakespeare's grasp of humanity or poetry, his troubling displays of power, and his wonderful and delightful exposure of sexual identity, however much great acting companies, actors, and actresses produce staggering performances of his plays, Milton's interrogations of free will, liberty, and the threat to it are more riveting. No student of Milton has left *Paradise Lost* without feeling such an admiration, indeed an ardor of admiration.

Milton was born into a prosperous middle-class London family of Protestant and conformist views. He had the best education money could buy, at St. Paul's School, before studying at Christ's College, Cambridge, which he left after taking a B.A. in 1629 and an M.A. in 1632. Having put aside any thought of holy orders, he committed himself to a country retreat in order to study the art of being a poet, perhaps with an eye to future aristocratic or even royal patronage.

He did this with some success, and by 1640 had accumulated an impressive collection of poems. These ranged from the avant-garde in diction and prosody to workings out of the English idioms of Spenser, Shakespeare, and Jonson; to highly competent Latin elegies; to some daring Italian sonnets; to exquisite English poems on subjects including music, the power of the English vernacular, and the birth and death of Christ. There were also two phenomenal pieces that each radically transformed the genre in which they were written: *A Masque presented at Ludlow Castle, 1634* (usually called *Comus*) and the pastoral elegy *Lycidas*.

This left him a somewhat known poet with a secure reputation; he would undoubtedly have been remembered as a significant post-Spenserian poet of the 1630s had he died in 1640. But then came the civil crisis of the midcentury. Milton had toured Italy as a way of furthering his education and claimed that he returned in order to be of use to his countrymen in a time of unrest. Indeed, he wrote a series of pro-Puritan tracts against the bishops, in which he began to offer a view of the poet as a national savior—a prophet for the nation. These are intriguing examples of a masterful writer flexing his muscles as a polemicist and satirist. They also reveal Milton to be grappling with major issues of political, religious, and literary difference in his day—the first formulation of his insight that we struggle for truth through the apprehension of contrarieties in the materials in front of us.

Yet this was nothing compared to what happened next. In 1642, Milton married, and it was clearly an unhappy, incompatible match. His wife returned to her father's house, and Milton wrote a treatise in favor of divorce, against standard and hardly ever challenged precepts, using the astonishing argument that Christ's denial of divorce was consistent with Moses's permission for divorce. This staggering assertion outraged most divines and brought the author the unwelcome attention of Parliament. Milton had unwittingly garnered for himself the reputation of a religious radical and a moral libertine, and he may have published a collected edition of his poetry (much of what he had written up to 1645) in order to create an image of respectability.[2] More than that, it was in the divorce writings, with their assault on major assumptions in philosophy and theology, that some more fundamental beliefs emerged in Milton's mind—in particular the heresies of mortalism (the idea that the soul dies with the body until the general resurrection) and its anterior foundation, monism (the idea that everything in the universe is matter of some kind; there is no separation of the material and the immaterial, and no division of the soul and the body). The first divorce tract produced many hostile responses, which eventually compelled Milton to defend himself in three further tracts.

With Parliament introducing a book-licensing system of its own (after a long period of royal and church censorship and a brief period of press freedom), Milton defended freedom of the press in his famous *Areopagitica,* and in doing so offered the first mature version of his free-will theology: that if we are not allowed to choose between good and evil, we are alienating the image of God in us. *Areopagitica* had little or limited impact in the weeks immediately following its publication (its substantial fame followed fifty years later and thereafter), but it has the same energy, the same sense of contradiction, the voice of dissent as well as the voice of orthodoxy, that are present in the divorce tracts. All these tracts embody the sense of having read enormous amounts of printed material, to the extent that we feel the mind of the writer about to explode under the pressure of confronting it. In the space of about two years, three at the most, Milton had undergone several intellectual revolutions, and he had formulated theories of domestic and civil reformation that he thought went along with the parliamentarian and Puritan arguments for liberty from the king and his supporters. This body of work is Milton at his most optimistic; everything that followed bears in some sense the mark of compromise and disappointment. In being the intellectual rebel, Milton had also discovered the voice of Satan; he would nurture it in the following years of retirement and exile from the center of power, as he remade Western poetry in his great epic and its two sequel works and as he cast his continuing and unfading interrogation of liberty's dimensions within those works. In several ways, rebellion is figured positively in Milton's great statements of the 1640s, but it returned in the complicated darkness of both Satan and Samson, characters from texts that were completed when Milton had been cast aside and was treated officially with contempt. The oscillation of sympathy back and forth between Milton's narrator and Satan is a further measure of the contradiction and chaos that underwrote this experience.

Milton is an author for all Americans, whether conservative, liberal, or radical, not only because he was a favorite of the founding fathers, so that his voice echoes through their writings, but also because his visionary writing is a literary embodiment of so many of the aspirations that have guided Americans as they have sought to establish lived ideals of ethical and spiritual perfection. The resonance of his themes of liberty and deliverance has appealed to African-Americans like Eva Jessye, who cast *Paradise Lost* and *Paradise Regained* as spiritual songs in the 1920s. To a large extent reading Milton requires engagement with rebellion, most fully embodied in the characters of Satan, the other rebel angels, and Adam and Eve and in the sense of rejection of the customary and the enslaving. After all, Milton wrote in support of a regicide. Necessarily there is substantial sympathetic engagement with characters and forms of intelligence regarded as conventionally "evil"—natural-born killers, so to speak—and an unending resistance to imposed authority and an attempt to build a world that happily embraces these contrary energies. Milton knew and loved Renaissance drama; he picks up the heretical dynamism of Christopher Marlowe's compelling characters and makes much more of them, and in doing so he also moves far beyond the doubts that define but also limit Hamlet.

This book thus argues strongly against the two influential contentions of Stanley Fish: first, in *Surprised by Sin: The Reader in Paradise Lost*, that Milton was trying to induce sinful thoughts in his readers so that he could then teach them the error of their ways; and second, more recently, in *How Milton Works,* that Milton is the apologist for an ultimately theological and contained view of life. Milton's celebration of contrariness and chaotic, various energy makes his art and thought escape from such limited descriptions and is peculiarly resonant with our own moment, and with the youth art of the past four decades. Milton's art builds by pulling down. It is no surprise that one contemporary writer who has unashamedly made capital of Miltonic incarnations and themes, Philip Pullman (especially in the His Dark Materials trilogy), has enjoyed enormous international literary success. Or that *Paradise Lost* should so run through the narrative and visual dynamics of Neil Gaiman's intelligent and brooding Sandman comic books. Or that themes of a challenge to oppressive organized religion delivered in "holy-war imagery" and with lyrics referring to psychological and physical mutilation in such circumstances should run through the work of the Grammy-winning metal band Slayer. Furthermore, Milton's insights into the possibilities and limitations of scientific discovery chime with both our quest for knowledge and our now certain knowledge that we have damaged our world with our technology. Milton is an indubitably ecological poet in ways that our forefathers did not see, and his perceptiveness about the natural world is bound up with his heterodoxy.[3]

Yet far from being the apostle of human limitation and the poet of a bigoted faith, Milton had an intense belief in the primacy of personal interpretations of the Bible that produced a vision of divine and human potential which is always reassessing its own foundations in a critical refusal of fixed and absolute standards of truth. Some would argue that Milton is already a postreligious writer—not a position that can readily be accepted except insofar as religion is defined as subservience to the authority and traditions of a church. Milton wants each person to think out truth for himself; heresy for Milton is a good thing. It is a vision that embraces the faithful and those who proclaim no faith, and its significance stems in large part from its thoughtful associations with both camps and draws them under one umbrella, encouraging them to deploy their rational powers as never before. Milton did not approve of blasphemy, but he did conceive of education and mental reflection as an ever-expanding, ever-self-revising project of interaction between person and world. The applications of his vision in a multicultural and multiethnic context have been overlooked; the capacity of his writings to facilitate cross-cultural mutual understanding has not yet been fully realized. It might be noted that Milton and his followers in Anglo-American tradition stand contrary to Leo Strauss and his followers (despite attempts by Straussians to co-opt Milton), whose elitist and authoritarian ideas are seen by many as having had a detrimental effect on intellectual life and on the current administration in particular. Straussians have tried to prove that there is a hidden and authoritarian truth in Milton; this study rebuts that position. Most serious Miltonists try to aspire to the poet's remarkable learning, but the truths in Milton, various and liberal, are there for all to see.

Much is said of the United States having lost its way. Furthermore, the Anglo-American "special relationship" has reasserted the theme of the "white man's burden" in its Middle Eastern and Asian policies but has been deeply compromised by the outcomes of its actions in these regions and by the response of West Europeans, Britons, and Americans to their governments. In terms appropriate to his own day but that are readily understandable and applicable in our own, Milton warned of matters of this kind and built a response to them in his poetry. Reading Milton as he should be read is one path of restitution, not of consolation but of continued and better engagement; the pages that follow suggest a way to that path. As our experience of preeminence mutates into something else, Milton's particular treatment of loss and defeat, as well as of the complicatedness of positive potential, will be a crucial, prescient tool of reflection, a strong recommendation for the virtue of his poetry.

1

POETICS AND POETIC STRATEGIES

When I first read Milton's verse, I couldn't think what to say about it. I was seventeen; *Paradise Lost* was a required text in high school, but we avoided it. Instead I read a short poem by Milton in Helen Gardner's *Metaphysical Poets* anthology. Donne, Herbert, and Marvell, for instance, were interestingly tortuous because they wrote in conceits and you had to figure them out. Not so Milton: the poetry is there in front of you, literally saying what it means. "At a Solemn Music" (ca. 1633) would be an example:

> Blest pair of sirens, pledges of heaven's joy,
> Sphere-borne harmonious sisters, Voice, and Verse,
> Wed your divine sounds, and mixed power employ
> Dead things with inbreathed sense able to pierce,
> And to our high-raised phantasy present,

That undisturbed song of pure concent,
Ay sung before the sapphire-coloured throne
To him that sits thereon
With saintly shout, and solemn jubilee,
Where the bright seraphim in burning row
Their loud uplifted angel trumpets blow,
And the cherubic host in thousand choirs
Touch their immortal harps of golden wires,
With those just spirits that wear victorious palms,
Hymns devout and holy psalms
Singing everlastingly;
That we on earth with undiscording voice
May rightly answer that melodious noise;
As once we did, till disproportioned sin
Jarred against nature's chime, and with harsh din
Broke the fair music that all creatures made
To their great Lord, whose love their motion swayed
In perfect diapason, whilst they stood
In first obedience, and their state of good.
O may we soon again renew that song,
And keep in tune with heaven, till God ere long
To his celestial consort us unite,
To live with him, and sing in endless morn of light.

(*CSP*, 167–170)

The poem is about perfection, and evokes a capella singing (a mixture of voice and verse) as a force that brings dead things to life and gives the listener an image of God on a sapphire throne, at the center of massed angelic choirs. The heavenly vision will draw more song from humans. Adam and Eve sang so, but sin, a principle of disharmony, interrupted. The poem calls for a renewal of that song, so that we can all again be part of that large heavenly choir. It is extremely heady stuff, presenting music as capable of producing an ecstasy by appealing to the mind's faculty of fantasy. The Italian madrigal form is exquisite in itself, and the rhythm in the phrasing and meter is just remarkable; nothing is out of place. At the same time, the world of discord is implied by negative implication: "undisturbed," "undiscorded."

What is intriguing about the poem's effect is that it wants to take you right there to God, and to what Milton imagines the experience of heaven to be. There is no messing with human frailty or the mortification that human sinfulness requires, no humbling before the cross. This is also true of Milton's unfinished poem "The Passion" (? March 1630), which rejects the image of the crucifixion as an inappropriate poetic confinement. Instead there follows a description of the poet-prophet asking to be whisked to Jerusalem in a chariot like Ezekiel's in order to have a better vision of the crucified Christ and to write verse on the tomb at Gethsemane. The poem ceases, unable to proceed, largely, I suspect, because the poet cannot imagine where to fly next—or he is repressed at this point. The sixth stanza gives it all away: Ezekiel's vision was of a chariot in heaven, and the implication is that that poet-prophet wants a chariot to take him there:

> See see the chariot, and those rushing wheels,
> That whirled the prophet up at Chebar flood,
> My spirit some transporting cherub feels,
> To bear me where the towers of Salem stood,
> Once glorious towers, now sunk in guiltless blood;
>   There doth my soul in holy vision sit
> In pensive trance, and anguish, and ecstatic fit.
>
> ("The Passion," *CSP*, 125)

The demotion of the cross is a Protestant reflex, or rather a Puritan one, but equally interesting is the doubleness of that sixth stanza. The depiction of prophetic transport promises more than the destination we are given. And there are other ways in which this complexity works: the destination is Jerusalem, literal and historic, but Protestantism never entirely escaped from the pre-reformed allegorical interpretation of the holy city as a figure for the church generally and, more importantly, as heaven.

The stanza form is shared with the finished "On the Morning of Christ's Nativity" (25 December 1629), which transports the reader through Christ's impact in the universe and through time (rapidly leaving behind the iconography of the nativity scene in the stable). The diction and rhyme are remarkably precise, following an Italian *canzone* pattern that had already been used by Spenser and the underrated Scottish poet Drummond of Hawthornden. Typically in early Milton, Italianate form (and echoes of authors such as Petrarch) is articulated through consciously English poetic vocabulary. In this case, much from Spenser, Shakespeare, Chapman, and others is being reworked and represented as a refined purity. The poetry cleanses the senses. Milton was also interested in the terms of Italian literary theory, as well as in the best examples of its practice, in particular the idea of *versi sciolti* ("loose," "unbounded," or "nimble" poetry; the term is now used for blank verse). He later mentioned the idea of a ductile verse, muscular in its nature, in the preface to *Paradise Lost*. There is plentiful rhyme throughout his early poetry, but the sense of chime matched by appropriate syllables, carrying the meaning in an unimpeded way, is typical: "apt numbers, fit quantity of syllables, and the sense variously drawn out from one verse into another."

Like many young men in the early seventeenth century, Milton would have had his first sustained experience of poetry in Latin. Competence in Latin was encouraged at school and then university by regular exercises in Latin verse composition. Several of Milton's early Latin poems began in this way, and those in English were translations from Latin. Here is one source of a prosody in which the counting of syllables matters more than rhyme (since Latin verse does not rhyme). By his eighteenth year, Milton was capable of writing exquisite long Latin verse, and by his twenty-first year he was composing seriously competent Italian sonnets (which did rhyme). Milton was a polyglot poet, ultimately aiming to glorify his native tongue by writing an epic in it but always thinking through the resources of several literary languages—Greek, Latin, Italian, later on some Hebrew—and sending their presence into English.

There are many aspects of the early Latin poetry that make it worth reading even in English translation. The sheer level of competence demonstrated in writing Latin verse is one feature, and another, of more thematic importance, is the figures who speak and who are therefore given a distinctive voice in the elegies: the very subjects who are being mourned. It is here that Milton can be seen investing in the kind of prophetic voice that would be so crucial in later years; see, for instance, *Elegia III. On the Death of the Bishop of Winchester* (September–December 1626). But if Milton was to succeed as an English poet, he would have to make all of the ability he had developed in his youth in various languages come to rest in an English poetry that equaled or superseded the best English verse of his day. That poetry was to be found in the English drama, with Shakespeare as its jewel and Ben Jonson not far behind, and in the 1630s Englishmen dared to say that with Shakespeare, their literature outshone the classics.

Milton found his way forward into a new realm of competence in writing his first great work, *A Masque presented at Ludlow Castle 1634,* or *Comus.* This was his second commissioned entertainment, written in 1634 and deeply indebted to but developing the lyrical and theatrical achievements of Shakespeare, Jonson, and John Fletcher. *Comus* makes description of ethereal and terrestrial realms out of ancient and English sources, but it does so in a way that is intrinsically responsive to the claims of different levels of experience, deriving from the senses and the intellect, as it tells its story of chaste resistance to the temptation of lustful corruption. Each line of verse is a poetic embodiment of the moralized universe of the masque, and at its heart is sensuous temptation and the beginnings of an interrogation of the problematic interrelatedness of the physical body and the mind or soul. The character Comus thus offers a kind of rap poetry against the sobriety of the Lady and the Attendant Spirit:

> Mean while welcome joy, and feast,
> Midnight shout, and revelry,
> Tipsy dance, and jollity.
> Braid your locks with rosy twine
> Dropping odours, dropping wine.
> Rigour now is gone to bed,
> And Advice with scrupulous head,
> Strict Age, and sour Severity,
> With their grave saws in slumber lie.
>
> (lines 102–110, *CSP*, 186)

The sense of musical grandeur and ecstasy-inducing verse reaches new levels of accomplishment when *Comus* manages to synthesize two contrary poetic modes Milton had established, the upbeat and the melancholy (first respectively embodied in his poems "L'Allegro" and "Il Penseroso"). In a truly intellectually challenging way, grandeur is accomplished in *Lycidas* (November 1637), in which Milton tackled a severely difficult subject, the death of an ac-

quaintance (Edward King), and found the problem of naming grief
energizing:

> Where were ye nymphs when the remorseless deep
> Closed o'er the head of your loved Lycidas?
> For neither were ye playing on the steep,
> Where your old bards, the famous Druids, lie,
> Nor on the shaggy top of Mona high,
> Nor yet where Deva spreads her wizard stream:
> Ay me, I fondly dream!
> Had ye been there . . . for what could that have done?
> What could the muse herself that Orpheus bore,
> The muse her self for her enchanting son
> Whom universal nature did lament,
> When by the rout that made the hideous roar,
> His gory visage down the stream was sent,
> Down the swift Hebrus to the Lesbian shore.

> (lines 50–63, *CSP*, 246–247)

The embodiment of grief in line 57, where the sense changes
abruptly halfway through the line, adds a new voice of personal engagement. It was probably a surprise to have the poem resolve itself
in the dread voice of Saint Peter's prophecy, which blames Lycidas's
death on the bishops of the Church of England. The poem is thus a
lament that becomes a complaint and so remakes its genre entirely.

But this is as nothing compared with *Paradise Lost*'s ability to give
the sense that the words *are* what they describe:

> Thus saying, from her side the fatal key,
> Sad instrument of all our woe, she took;
> And towards the gate rolling her bestial train,
> Forthwith the huge portcullis high updrew,
> Which but herself, not all the Stygian powers
> Could once have moved; then in the key-hole turns
> The intricate wards, and every bolt and bar
> Of massy iron or solid rock with ease
> Unfastens: on a sudden open fly
> With impetuous recoil and jarring sound
> The infernal doors, and on their hinges grate
> Harsh Thunder, that the lowest bottom shook
> Of Erebus. She opened, but to shut
> Excelled her power; the gates wide open stood,
> That with extended wings a bannered host
> Under spread ensigns marching might pass through
> With horse and chariots ranked in loose array;
> So wide they stood, and like a furnace mouth
> Cast forth redounding smoke and ruddy flame.

(II.871–889)

Sin is opening the gates of hell, enabling Satan to escape to the earth. Milton produces a unique soundscape for this description. The *o* sounds in lines 872–874 underline the sense of woe for mankind that this event entails; the gates of hell, closed by the portcullis, the mouth of the beast Sin, and all the mouths you can think of sounding *o* suggest a huge wailing or devouring mouth. Then the revolving motion of the key turning suggests that which ought to be reversible (keys can be used to lock again), but we learn that Sin was not strong enough to lock the gate. Some revolutions are irreversible. The emblematic associations of the keywords also evoke a doubleness that is similar to contrariness, but this time it helps the informed reader understand that there is a better world somewhere else. The "fatal key" is the opposite of the "key of life" that opens the gates of death. The "woe" of the opening portcullis is replaced by the jarring and grating of the gate as it swings, likened to the sound of artillery ordinance ("impetuous recoil"), in opposition to the harmoniously moving gates of heaven (VII.205–207). But then the open mouth returns at the end of the passage: "*o*pened," the wide-open gates gape, large enough to allow an army to pass, a gaping mouth belching fire and smoke. All the time the "sense variously drawn out" is marching the reader's attention onward, turning over the ends of the iambic lines, as the key turns in the lock, balanced by the caesurae within each line. "Fly" is attached at the end of line 879 to describe the following line, but it stands by itself for the moment before the reader's eye moves on to that next line, and "fly" by itself tells us about all the evil leaving hell with escape velocity.

That the style in *Paradise Lost* has often been likened to prose in poetry, a comparison enhanced by the marked lack of coincidence between sentence and line, draws our attention to the prose itself, and we confront a paradox. For *Of Reformation* (May 1641) is like a poem in prose. It is constructed like a Spenserian allegory of the evils of the Roman church. We are given a history of the church with England's special place in it—a quintessentially Protestant narrative—but Milton drives history with allegorical incarnations that whirl into sensual overload in long Ciceronian sentences:

> But to dwell no longer in characterizing the *depravities* of the *Church,* and how they sprung, and how they took increase; when I recall to mind at last, after so many dark ages, wherein the huge overshadowing train of *Error* had almost swept all the stars out of the firmament of the *Church;* how the bright and blissful *Reformation* (by divine power) strook through the black and settled night of *ignorance* and *antichristian tyranny,* me thinks a sovereign and reviving joy must needs rush into the bosom of him that reads or hears; and the sweet odour of the returning *Gospel* imbathe his soul with the fragrancy of Heaven. Then was the sacred BIBLE sought out of the dusty corners where profane Falsehood and Neglect had thrown it, the *schooles* opened, *divine* and *humane learning* raked out of the *embers* of *forgotten tongues,* the *princes* and *cities* trooping apace to the new erected banner of *salvation;* the *martyrs,* with the unresistable *might* of *weakness,* shaking the *powers* of *darkness,* and scorning the *fiery rage* of the old *red Dragon.*

> (*Of Reformation, CPW,* I.524–525)

At the same time, speaking against corruption involves a desecration of figures hitherto thought beyond reproach. It is the Christian martyrs who suffer Milton's ire in this tract, "for those who suffer silently without denouncing their persecutors lack zeal and invite the charge of vainglory." The author navigates across the body of history, ancient wisdom, and Christian scholarship to meet error head on and refute it in the name of truth. What appeared white is now black. And thus bishops (and one of them was the subject of a fine early Latin elegy by Milton) degenerate in the body of faith, so that they become offensive even to God:

> And it is still *episcopacy* that before all our eyes worsens and slugs the most learned, and seeming religious of our *ministers,* who no sooner advanced to it, but like a seething pot set to cool, sensibly exhale and reek out the greatest part of that zeal, and those gifts which were formerly in them, settling in a skinny congealment of ease and sloth at the top: and if they keep their learning by some potent sway of nature, 'tis a rare chance; but their *devotion* most commonly comes to that queasy temper of luke-warmness, that gives a vomit to GOD himself.
>
> (*Of Reformation, CPW,* I.536–537)

Yet the encounter with error perforce engenders confusion in the mind of the reformed writer, and a similar kind of confusion or chaos is created as a consequence of the defamation that was part of interconfessional polemic. In *Animadversions,* a slightly later antiepiscopal tract, of July 1641, Milton refers to *The Epistle Con-*

gratulatorie of Lysimachus Nicanor, a work in which the Anglican John Corbet pretended to be a Jesuit congratulating the Scottish Presbyterians and thereby suggesting that Catholics and Presbyterians were identical (*CPW,* I.667–668). In *Paradise Lost,* Chaos is the neutral place of contending elements that looks different depending on the perspective of whoever looks at it, be it Satan in Book II or Raphael in Book VII. In *The Reason of Church Government* (January-February 1642), the reference to chaos, contrariety, and reformation is followed by the image of dross and waste being the inevitable consequence of creation, and then by an attack in kind on the Scottish Catholic polemicist John Barclay for his assertion in *Icon Animorum* (1614) that the English lack manners. Milton casts Barclay as a wandering exile, "a fugitive Papist traducing the island whence he sprung" and therefore shunning the natural aversion to atheism in England (he was in fact born in France to a Scottish father). Barclay is figured as an outcast Satan; by leaving the island homeland, he exposes himself to the dangers that the church and education in England prevent—a further lapse from barbarous habits into error. It takes other nations, "better composed to a natural civility," to survive these threats without such nurture (*The Reason of Church Government, CPW,* I.796–797).

The subjection to chaos is not merely a way of registering a trial of faith. It is also the figure of reading, and of being open to all truths in order to choose freely. This takes us to the famous emendation in

Milton's own hand in early copies of *Areopagitica* (November 1644) of "wayfaring" to "warfaring" reader:

> And perhaps this is that doom which *Adam* fell into of knowing good and evil, that is to say of knowing good by evil. As therefore the state of man now is; what wisdom can there be to choose, what continence to forbear without the knowledge of evil? He that can apprehend and consider vice with all her baits and seeming pleasures, and yet abstain, and yet distinguish, and yet prefer that which is truly better, he is the true wayfaring Christian. I cannot praise a fugitive and cloistered virtue, unexercised and unbreathed, that never sallies out and sees her adversary, but slinks out of the race, where that immortal garland is to be run for, not without dust and heat. Assuredly we bring not innocence into the world, we bring impurity much rather: that which purifies us is trial, and trial is by what is contrary.
>
> (*Areopagitica, CPW,* II.514–515)

The set of associations just elaborated makes the originally printed reading, "wayfaring," as appropriate as the revision, "warfaring," which is usually preferred by modern scholars. It is not only in the character of Comus, then, that we see the origins of the character of Satan, but in Milton's experience as a scholar and a polemicist—something that will become obvious in the chapters that follow.

In *Of Reformation,* Milton presents poets' ability to "give a personal form to what they please" (that is, to engage in personification and allegory) as a special kind of perceptiveness, and the heroic English as the fit objects of "the heroic song of all POSTERITY" (*CPW,* I.585, 597). In the second part of *The Reason of Church Government,* Milton described his writings as the work of reformation, the poet being the national redeemer, distilling the best wisdom from ancient Israel, Greece, Rome, and modern Italy for the benefit of "mine own citizens throughout this island in the mother dialect" (*CPW,* I.812). Poets who make the wrong choice of decorum are as guilty of a moral lapse as those who neglect virtuous subject matter. Poetry should take its place, he says (again looking back to the public culture of the ancient city-states), in an array of public exercises that sharpen bodies and minds in the causes of justice, temperance, fortitude, and military preparedness. This amounts to an astonishing attack on one of the fundamental tenets of the art of poetry since ancient times, and one that was deeply embedded in the humanist tradition. According to Milton, not only is poetry regarded as an aspect of youthful ardor, amorousness, or drunkenness, to be put aside, but also the role of the art of memory as the chief means of inventing the subject matter of poetry is to be spurned. Instead, true poetry is driven by direct divine inspiration,

> nor to be obtained by the invocation of Dame Memory and her Siren daughters, but by devout prayer to that eternal spirit who can enrich with all utterance and knowledge, and sends out his seraphim with

the hallowed fire of his altar to touch and purify the lips of whom
he pleases.

(The Reason of Church Government, CPW, I.820–821)

In this frenzy, the poet, "soaring in the high region of his fancies with
his garland and singing robes about him," is not entirely divorced
from the prose writer, the two roles being famously described by Milton as respectively the right- and left-handed tasks of a single person
(*Of Reformation, CPW,* I.808).

Of Reformation seeks to purify the body of Christ and his church;
its method is a near-frenzied list of accumulated error, a good deal of
it denounced in the texts of Milton's favorite authors, such as the poets Dante, Petrarch, and Chaucer, and in texts Milton believed to be
by Chaucer. Milton's image of ideal perfection is the commonwealth
as much as the church:

> To be plainer Sir, how to solder, how to stop a leak, how to keep up
> the floating carcass of a crazy, and diseased monarchy, or state betwixt wind, and water, swimming still upon her own dead lees, that
> now is the deep design of a politician. Alas Sir! a commonwealth
> ought to be but as one huge Christian personage, one mighty growth,
> and stature of an honest man, as big, and compact in virtue as in
> body; for look what the grounds, and causes are of single happiness
> to one man, the same ye shall find them to a whole state, as Aristotle
> both in his ethics, and politics, from the principles of reason lays

down by consequence therefore, that which is good, and agreeable to monarchy, will appear soonest to be so, by being good, and agreeable to the true welfare of every Christian, and that which can be justly proved hurtful, and offensive to every true Christian, will be evinced to be alike hurtful to monarchy: for *God* forbid, that we should separate and distinguish the end, and good of a monarch, from the end and good of the monarchy, or of that, from Christianity.

(*Of Reformation, CPW,* I.572–573)

The perfected body is both image and reality, and the result of the vision of the inspired poet. Imagining how things ought to be is the province of this visionary form of personification. On the one hand, it enables Milton to argue with enormous rhetorical and polemical force (in this case for the integrity of a Christian monarchy), and on the other, it is a means for analyzing the elements that actually make up social and individual wholes: the matter of bodies and how they relate to one another.

Thus the quotation from *Of Reformation* I've just set out might be coupled with another, from *Eikonoklastes* ("The Image Breaker," October 1649), the attack on Charles I's posthumously published and jointly authored defense of himself, *Eikon Basilike* ("The King's Image"):

He ought then to have so thought of a Parliament, if he count it not male, as of his mother, which, to civil being, created both him and the royalty he wore. And if it hath bin anciently interpreted the presaging sign of a future tyrant, but to dream of copulation with his mother, what can it be less than actual tyranny to affirm waking, that the parliament, which is his mother, can neither conceive or bring forth any authoritative act without his masculine coition: nay that his reason is as celestial and life-giving to the parliament, as the sun's influence is to the earth: what other notions but these, or such like, could swell up Caligula to think himself a god?

(CPW, III.467)

The relationship between king and Parliament is thought through by reference to ancient history, in which dream interpretation played a prominent part. Incest becomes a figure of political impropriety and tyranny; lawmaking is improperly conceived by Charles as a kind of profoundly misplaced paternal insemination. Such imagery is not uncommon in 1640s political controversy, but the extent of Milton's fusion of different registers of meaning as he seeks to understand the body politic is of a high and consistent intelligibility. He is thinking politics in analogies and images—politics as a poet would have it.

A final example of this kind of writing is in *Areopagitica,* where the matter of free speech is connected to the final act of reformation in a gathering up of the lost body of truth:

Truth indeed came once into the world with her divine master, and was a perfect shape most glorious to look on: but when he ascended,

---

and his Apostles after Him were laid asleep, then strait arose a wicked race of deceivers, who as that story goes of the Egyptian Typhon with his conspirators, how they dealt with the good Osiris, took the virgin Truth, hewed her lovely form into a thousand pieces, and scattered them to the four winds. From that time ever since, the sad friends of Truth, such as durst appear, imitating the careful search that Isis made for the mangled body of Osiris, went up and down gathering up limb by limb still as they could find them. We have not yet found them all, Lords and Commons, nor ever shall do, till her master's second coming; he shall bring together every joint and member, and shall mould them into an immortal feature of loveliness and perfection.

(*CPW*, II.549)

Nearly every image in *Areopagitica* is complicated by an opposite somewhere else in the tract, and Milton does not comment on the implication in his source story of Isis and Osiris that Isis never found the genitalia of her dismembered partner; nonetheless, the fact is that the image of gathering truth dominates the literal background reference to licensing legislation in Parliament and takes the reader into extremely rarified realms of speculation.

This visionary richness is carried directly into Milton's great later poetry, where it makes possible a heroic poetry of embodiment that addresses on every level of content and style the meaning of the politics of bodies. Although *Paradise Lost* was supposed—so Milton claimed—to be an entirely literal history of the creation and fall of man, as opposed to the romance allegories of medieval and Renaissance literary tradition, there is frequent recourse to the figurative to enable the narration of the poem to take place. Raphael has to "liken spiritual unto corporal forms" in order for Adam and Eve to understand him. And thus embodiment becomes an object of fascination for the reader from the very start of the poem. What is the meaning of the vast dimensions of the body of Satan, as we meet him shortly after his fall, in Book I?

> Thus Satan talking to his nearest mate
> With head uplift above the wave, and eyes
> That sparkling blazed, his other parts besides
> Prone on the flood, extended long and large
> Lay floating many a rood, in bulk as huge
> As whom the fables name of monstrous size,
> Titanian, or Earth-born, that warred on Jove,
> Briareos or Typhon, whom the den
> By ancient Tarsus held, or that sea-beast
> Leviathan, which God of all his works
> Created hugest that swim the ocean stream:
> Him haply slumbering on the Norway foam
> The pilot of some small night-foundered skiff,
> Deeming some island, oft, as seamen tell,
> With fixed anchor in his scaly rind
> Moors by his side under the lee, while night

Invests the sea, and wishèd morn delays:
So stretched out huge in length the arch-fiend lay
Chained on the burning Lake, nor ever thence
Had risen or heaved his head, but that the will
And high permission of all-ruling Heaven
Left him at large to his own dark designs,
That with reiterated crimes he might
Heap on himself damnation, while he sought
Evil to others, and enraged might see
How all his malice served but to bring forth
Infinite goodness, grace and mercy shown
On Man by him seduced, but on himself
Treble confusion, wrath and vengeance poured.
Forthwith upright he rears from off the pool
His mighty stature; on each hand the flames
Driv'n backward slope their pointing spires, and, rolled
In billows, leave i' th' midst a horrid vale.

(I.192–224)

"Prone" (line 195) and "rood" (line 196) are in fact words associated with parts of unreformed church architecture, both being names for the screen between the nave and the chancel, and "prone" being particularly associated with the place where notices of excommunication were placed and hence where ecclesiastical tyranny, as Milton would have seen it, was exercised. The Old Testament sea monster of Job 41,

Leviathan, was associated with the devil, power, and sin, but by the mid-seventeenth century, Thomas Hobbes had made the monster famous as an image of the state. Hobbes's *Leviathan* (1651) and the theory of authoritarian sovereignty therein were anathema to everything Milton thought about the state. The echo is delicious and obvious to any informed contemporary reader. And these two points of explanation do no justice to the typically "perpendicular" prosody that marks the passage, as if the words were working in three dimensions. This includes first and foremost the huge poetic sentence that imitates the vastness of the serpent's tail and finishes with Satan's rebellion again implicitly invoked as he stands up in the lake of fire and as he does so leaves behind, also again, the gaping hole, like that at the mouth of hell, opened by Sin. The poem's potential for simultaneously personal and public speculation and analysis is both immediate and compelling. This is why *Paradise Lost* remains in the opinion of so many the greatest political poem in the language.

If *Paradise Lost* is a demonstration of fullness in language (in the case of Satan, the fullness of negativity and emptiness), the opposite is the case with the two late poems *Paradise Regained* and *Samson Agonistes* (1671).[1] The former deliberately eschews the rhetorical grandness of *Paradise Lost* in favor of the "still small voice" (1 Kings 19:12). Long epic similes dealing in astonishing spatial and temporal dimensions are replaced by figures of grammar, including repetition. Image and vision are replaced by reasoning, as the entire poem is explicitly preoccupied by one question: Who is the Son of God? Argument in Miltonic style is everything in this poem:

> To whom our Saviour sternly thus replied.
> Deservedly thou griev'st, composed of lies
> From the beginning, and in lies wilt end;
> Who boast'st release from hell, and leave to come
> Into the heaven of heavens; thou com'st indeed,
> As a poor miserable captive thrall,
> Comes to the place where he before had sat
> Among the prime in splendour, now deposed,
> Ejected, emptied, gazed, unpitied, shunned,
> A spectacle of ruin or of scorn
> To all the host of heaven; the happy place
> Imparts to thee no happiness, no joy,
> Rather inflames thy torment, representing
> Lost bliss, to thee no more communicable,
> So never more in hell than when in heaven.
>
> (*Paradise Regained,* I.406–420, *CSP,* 440)

The poem is an answer to *Paradise Lost,* the New Testament to its Old. While it provides seemingly neat conclusions to issues that were vexing and indeterminable in *Paradise Lost,* it is at the same time more confidently conscious of reaching out to Milton's fellow Puritans and republicans, now discountenanced and in many cases suffering religious persecution. This is done most obviously by a series of references to biblical figures and texts that were identified with aspects of the Puritan movement.

But any thought that Milton was finally rendering an easy solution are dashed, first by the astonishing denunciation of classical learning in Book IV, lines 221–364, pretty much an attack on most of Milton's learning, then by the poem or drama with which *Paradise Regained* was first published in 1671, *Samson Agonistes*. In contrast to *Paradise Regained, Samson Agonistes* pursues violent solutions in a violent world. Line length varies, rhyme cuts in unexpectedly, and the diction is markedly literal and brutal. No doubt this was done to evoke the harsh world of the ancient Israelites in the Book of Judges and to suggest the feel of a resurrected ancient tragedy, or tragedy purified as Milton believed it should be. Nothing much seems to happen or change until we learn from the messenger that Samson has pulled down the pillars and killed the Philistine elite and himself with them. But in fact the drama is arranged as a series of confrontations between Samson and his antagonists—Manoa, his father; Dalila; and Harapha, the Philistine champion—in which debate is overtaken by the rhetorical force of Samson's words, and he more or less blows his second two interlocutors offstage with the violence of his rhetoric:

> *Sam.* No man withholds thee, nothing from thy hand
>   Fear I incurable; bring up thy van,
>   My heels are fettered, but my fist is free.

Har. This insolence other kind of answer fits.
Sam. Go baffled coward, lest I run upon thee,

> Though in these chains, bulk without spirit vast,
> And with one buffet lay thy structure low,
> Or swing thee in the air, then dash thee down
> To the hazard of thy brains and shattered sides.

Har. By Astaroth ere long thou shalt lament

> These braveries in irons loaden on thee.

Chor. His giantship is gone somewhat crestfall'n,

> Stalking with less unconscionable strides,
> And lower looks, but in a sultry chafe.

(lines 1233–1246, *CSP,* 398–399)

What kind of violence this might be, or what the uses of violence are, is a question put incessantly to the reader, most intensely in the central exchange with Dalila, in which the meaning of loyalty across private and public divides is raised. In this respect, we are again in the company of political values, as Dalila clearly represents loyalty to nationhood, civil duty, and public religion ("the Priest/Was . . . ever at my ear,/. . . what had I/To oppose against such powerful arguments?" [lines 857–858, 861–862, *CSP,* 386]). Samson, the private man, is God's chosen, out of favor and certain that he must respond when the moment comes ("Be of good courage, I begin to feel/Some rousing motions in me which dispose/To something extraordinary my thoughts" [lines 1381–1383]) but uncertain of the consequences.

The violent conclusion has brought the controversial charge that

Samson is Milton's picture of a terrorist, validating action by oppressed minorities against oppressive enemy states, which makes for uncomfortable speculation.[2] The play is also an act of imaginative violent aesthetic purging. Just as Milton implicitly criticizes the classical tradition in *Paradise Lost,* so in *Samson Agonistes* he trashes recognizably English, even Shakespearian theatrical incarnations (Manoa/Polonius; Dalila/Cleopatra; Harapha/Hotspur), all of whom are summoned only to be sent away from the stage by Samson, who cancels himself as a theatrical incarnation when he pulls down the theater (not the "house" of the Book of Judges, or the temple) and takes his own life as well as the those of the Philistines. What is left is the aftertaste of redefinition, as puzzling and memorable as his life and end were absorbingly energetic:

> he though blind of sight,
> Despised and thought extinguished quite,
> With inward eyes illuminated
> His fiery virtue roused
> From under ashes into sudden flame,
> And as an evening dragon came,
> Assailant on the perched roosts,
> And nests in order ranged
> Of tame villatic fowl; but as an eagle
> His cloudless thunder bolted on their heads.
> So virtue given for lost,

> Depressed, and overthrown, as seemed,
> Like that self-begotten bird
> In the Arabian woods embossed,
> That no second knows nor third,
> And lay erewhile a holocaust.

(lines 1687–1702, CSP, 411–412)

There is no writer who has in this way so bravely, and in old age so freshly and so astutely, entirely reframed his aesthetic and political agenda(s). In these late lines from his magnificent drama, Milton is telling us that he knows exactly what he has done.

2

DIVORCE

I

Sexuality is never absent from Milton's poetry. It is present in the early verse, for instance when, in *Lycidas*, there are some famous comments on the fear of sexual dalliance as a blight on poetic energy: "Were it not better done as others use,/To sport with Amaryllis in the shade,/Or with the tangles of Neaera's hair?" (lines 67–69). Hair is a mark of strength in men (witness Milton's Saint Peter in *Lycidas* and Samson) and of potential danger in women (witness Neaera and Eve), not least because it is erotically alluring. It wasn't just hair. Menstruation is an interest too, as when the younger Milton, still only twenty-five, has Comus, in the rhetorical guise of a divine, suggest that the Lady is unwilling to succumb to him and drink his draft because it is the "wrong time of the month." She is put off by the "lees/And settlings of a melancholy blood" (lines 808–809), a reference in the medical

---

language of the day to menstruation.[1] Even as an elderly man, Milton presents the Fall of man in *Paradise Lost* as situated between two moments of sexual utopianism. First is Milton's unconventional but not unprecedented view, expounded openly and literally when we first meet Adam and Eve, that there was coition in Paradise:

> nor turned I ween
> Adam from his fair spouse, nor Eve the rites
> Mysterious of connubial love refused:
> Whatever hypocrites austerely talk
> Of purity and place and innocence,
> Defaming as impure what God declares
> Pure, and commands to some, leaves free to all.
> Our maker bids increase, who bids abstain
> But our destroyer, foe to God and man?
> Hail wedded love, mysterious law, true source
> Of human offspring, sole propriety,
> In Paradise of all things common else.
> By thee adulterous lust was driven from men
> Among the bestial herds to range, by thee
> Founded in reason, loyal, just, and pure,
> Relations dear, and all the charities
> Of father, son, and brother first were known.
>
> (IV.741–757)

Then there is the joyous vision of angelic sex imparted by Raphael in Book VIII—frictionless sex involving the occupation of one angelic being by another. Gender is absent in this description, although the angels all seem, I think, to be men:

> Let it suffice thee that thou knowst
> Us happy, and without love no happiness.
> Whatever pure thou in the body enjoyst
> (And pure thou wert created) we enjoy
> In eminence, and obstacle find none
> Of membrane, joint, or limb, exclusive bars:
> Easier than air with air, if spirits embrace,
> Total they mix, union of pure with pure
> Desiring; nor restrained conveyance need
> As flesh to mix with flesh, or soul with soul.

(VIII.620–629)

Adam and Eve are also told by Raphael that they will become something like angels if they remain pure. This was clearly a good deal.

While Milton eschews conventional forms of sexual ardor, as he would have known it from courtly literature, and probably also an Italianate literature that praised the courtesan, he puts a very high premium on the special delights of sex (physical sex, that is) in marriage. The examples in *Paradise Lost* suggest that this is over and against the view that sex was tainted with original sin and therefore a necessity only for the purposes of reproduction. Milton's own sexual innocence (I take it he remained a virgin until he married) can be viewed many times in the early verse. The wonderful, fascinating, and dangerous world of *Comus* (1637), indebted to the most imaginative of the ancient Roman poets, Ovid, may be read as a theoretical treatise on the dangers of sex outside of marriage (as the Lady preaches chastity as sex within marriage throughout). It is a work on the cusp of sexual experience; the poet is yearning to be one of the experienced and excited, although officially repelled, by the sexual energies he finds in Comus. The Lady emanates the power of chastity, especially in her startling song, which arouses Comus's desire, reminding us of Angelo in Shakespeare's *Measure for Measure:* "Dost thou desire her foully for those things/That make her good?" We cannot quite tell where the "gums of glutinous heat" that make the Lady stick in her chair (after her brothers have forced Comus to flee but without ending his magic) come from—herself, Comus, or somewhere else. All we are sure of is that they seem very hot, sticky, and, frankly, spermatic—a further indication of Milton's refusal or inability to confront these issues.

Experience was not long in arriving. It was clearly all very difficult, and perhaps there is no better way of putting it than to say that Milton's uncomfortable experience at the beginning of his first marriage persuaded him to rethink the grounds on which marriage was made. The conventional view of marriage, widely taught throughout Christendom and repeated in the passage from *Paradise Lost,* Book IV, quoted above, was that marriage was for procreation. Milton instead argues that marriage is for "fit conversation," by which he meant that the woman was there to fill a lack in man, so avoiding the "evil of solitary life" (*The Doctrine and Discipline of Divorce, CPW,* II.235). If such a conversation was impossible—that is, if the partners were, as we would put it, incompatible—then divorce was a remedy. That, Milton says, was the point of Moses's permission for divorce in the Old Testament.

In a startling second move, a tremendous reversal of traditional teaching that comes at the beginning of the second book in *The Doctrine and Discipline of Divorce* (February 1644), Milton says that Christ's apparent denial of divorce for any cause apart from fornication is consistent with Moses's permission for divorce, because Christ meant by "fornication" those very differences of personality that compromised a fit conversation. There's a strong element of contrary logic in the argument. Given that there will be incompatible marriages, God cannot have denied divorce, because otherwise he would be legislating for adultery, which is, as it were, giving an evil to mankind. Milton is also highly purist in that he discounts all attempts to permit strictly limited divorce (through dispensations and "politick laws") as contrary to the simple hold that Mosaic permission still has over us, since it was never abrogated. Marriage in early modern Europe was also a fundamental part of economic systems, and insofar as it involved transferences of property was one of the key social binding factors in that world, but Milton does not mention this once.

We might be thinking of incompatibility in terms of emotional incompatibility, which in the seventeenth century would probably have been called spiritual incompatibility. But we have to remember that Milton was drawing his argument from Old Testament language, which takes us to the cause for divorce being "uncleanness":

> But in the Hebrew it sounds *nakedness of ought, or any real nakedness;* which by all the learned interpreters is referred to the mind, as well as to the body. And what greater nakedness or unfitness of mind then that which hinders ever the solace and peaceful society of the married couple, and what hinders that more then the unfitness and defective- ness of an unconjugal mind? The cause therefore of divorce expressed in the position cannot but agree with that described in the best and equalest sense of *Moses* Law. Which being a matter of pure charity, is plainly moral, and more now in force then ever: therefore surely lawful.
>
> (*The Doctrine and Discipline of Divorce, CPW,* II.244)

Milton wants to focus on the mind here, but the force of the Hebrew original compels him to take in the body too. And while he pursues the matter of incompatible partners, his descriptions of failed mar- riages take on very physical dimensions. Incompatibility might drive a man to extremes, "to piece up his lost contentment by visiting the stews, or stepping to his neighbour's bed, which is the common shift in this misfortune, or else by suffering his useful life to waste away and be lost under a secret affliction of an unconscionable size to human strength" (*The Doctrine and Discipline of Divorce, CPW,* II.247). Incompatibility is figured as a horrific travesty of sex: "to grind in the mill of an undelighted and servile copulation, must be the only forced work of a Christian marriage, oft times with such a yokefellow" (*The Doctrine and Discipline of Divorce, CPW,* II.258). Worse still, it is like being chained to a corpse (*The Doctrine and Discipline of Divorce, CPW,* II.326). There's a sense of intimacy as well as experience in this: "While it seems more moved at the disappointing of an impetuous nerve, then at the ingenuous grievance of a mind unreasonably yoked; and to place more of marriage in the channel of concupiscence, then in the pure influence of peace and love, whereof the souls lawful contentment is the only fountain" (*The Doctrine and Discipline of Divorce, CPW,* II.249).

Milton reads as if he were rather mixed up or inconsistent on the issue. On the one hand, marriage is not merely for procreation; on the other hand, the extent of the mutuality that marriage should afford extends to sexual relations, which is a part of mutuality, a complex mixture of the different spheres of human operation. In some places he assumes the conventionally accepted dualism of body and soul, which is present throughout his early writings, and in others the view that he was beginning to accept, monism, that body and soul were one and were continuous. On the one hand he is prepared to entertain Platonic mythology (Love is the son of Plenty and Poverty), where it is consistent with Mosaic teaching that love is the son of loneliness,[2] and on the other he is at pains to dismiss the Platonic idealism (the myth that lovers are two halves of an originally unitary soul) that works against his monism. The tension is to be seen in the uneasiness of *The Doctrine and Discipline of Divorce,* which is evident even on the level of composition. Thus Milton explains mutuality: "All ingenuous men will see that the dignity and blessing of marriage is placed rather in the mutual enjoyment of that which the wanting soul needfully seeks, then of that which the plenteous body would joyfully give away" (*The Doctrine and Discipline of Divorce, CPW,* II.252). But he corrected "joyfully" to "jollily," since "joys" connote sperm, and in "joyfully" he had a pun that would make the body too conscious of its own enjoyment and its procreative function. "Jollily" implies something more unthinking. However we approach the sentence, the dualism/monism confusion is apparent, and Milton appears to be divided against himself.

The divorce tracts search for terms that will make sense of Milton's perceptions. Without mutuality, "there can be left of wedlock nothing, but the empty husk of an outside matrimony" (*The Doctrine and Discipline of Divorce, CPW,* II.256), using an Old Testament dualism between the husk and the kernel (Num. 6:4). We should not try to "glue" together that which God and nature will not join—a rather clumsy word, and inadvertently revealing, since Comus stuck the Lady to the seat with the "gums of glutinous heat," often interpreted, as we have seen, as a reference to a spermatic substance. The most inherently contradictory moment comes in Chapter X of *The Doctrine and Discipline of Divorce*, where, in the context of a discussion of the need to avoid "mis-yoked" marriages, Milton lights on the word "cleave," which at once means both coming together ("a man will cleave to his like," Eccl. 13:16) and splitting apart. The implication feeds into Milton's understanding of the state of nature and the operation of seeds therein. It is fixated with the idea of contrariness:

> Seeing then there is indeed a twofold seminary or stock in nature, from whence are derived the issues of love and hatred distinctly flowing through the whole mass of created things, and that Gods doing ever is to bring the due likenesses and harmonies of his works together, except when out of two contraries met to their own destruction, he moulds a third existence.
>
> (*The Doctrine and Discipline of Divorce, CPW,* II.272)

This interesting possibility of a "third existence" produced out of contraries is not explored beyond its identification as "error" (it will reappear in *Areopagitica*), but Milton has reached an important point in his awareness thus far. Divorce, like creation, is a principle in nature, and its operation is originally a divine remit: "God and nature signifies and lectures to us not only by those recited decrees [such as the Ten Commandments], but even by the first and last of all his visible works; when by his divorcing command the world first rose out of chaos, nor can be renewed again out of confusion but by the separating of unmeet consorts" (*The Doctrine and Discipline of Divorce, CPW,* II.273). Did you hear that? He said, "Creation is divorce," and that divorces will have to happen before the world is rid of confusion.

There is a religious and political dimension to this reworking of the terms of marriage. An unmutual marriage is an idolatrous one, introducing religious delinquency into the home. It may also lead to atheism, or to the proliferation of sects. Evident here is the extent to which Puritan thinking had sanctified the home, creating in the theory of marriage something that would resemble a modern house church, with a very large extent of life's activities taken up inside the realm of the holy. Milton was living in London in the early 1640s, working as a schoolmaster, and clearly in touch with other Puritans who were finding the new order of Presbyterianism offensive. He found himself in the company of sectarian Puritans who, like him, were busy redescribing the central aspects of theology and social theory according to their own interpretations of the Bible. It is in these circles that different understandings of domestic relations were likely to occur. Charges of sexual impropriety, or free love, were commonly made against sectarians, and sometimes they were true.[3] Milton's *The Doctrine and Discipline of Divorce* bears textual echoes of one of the most startling pieces of sectarian theology in the period, *Man's Mortalitie,* an argument for the mortality of the soul, by the General

Baptist and future Leveller Richard Overton. It's hard to tell who read whom first, and we do not know if the two men knew each other (it is impossible that they did not know about each other, as their two books were listed together as abhorrent pieces of arch-heresy). Overton's mortalism was a means for Milton to find his own way of explaining his developing theory of "one flesh" in marriage.[4]

The Doctrine and Discipline of Divorce was revised and augmented in its second edition, of February 1644, but the furor it created caused Milton to defend his position by appealing to other reformers who shared his views as they attacked the Roman Catholic canon law on marriage: Grotius, Paulus Fagius, and especially Martin Bucer, from whose views Milton extracted quotations and upon whom he commented. *Tetrachordon* and *Colasterion* appeared on 4 March 1645. The former was an attempt to spend more time on a scriptural defense of his tenets. *Colasterion* was a riposte to an attack on *The Doctrine and Discipline, An Answer to a Book,* of November 1644, and shows seething contempt for its opponent's alleged lack of learning. One of its satirical registers is its invocation of domestic violence, of husband beating up wife. The divorce concern mutates by the time of *De Doctrina Christiana* (begun in 1655) into a reiteration, within the province of a man's private duties, of clear wifely duties owed to a husband and of certain Hebraic taboos for men to observe: for instance, avoidance of adultery, fornication, and intercourse with menstruating women. Female disobedience is wrong, because the woman literally comes from the body of the man. Milton also defended the legality of polygamy, since it had been practiced by the Old Testament patriarchs, and in this he follows a sporadic interest of earlier reformers.

II

These views are tested in *Paradise Lost.* Book IV presents Adam and Eve as exemplars of the mutuality that Milton idealizes in the divorce tracts. It is reported that Adam chased Eve when he first saw her, but unlike such chases in classical literature, which ended in rape, Adam chases Eve to have a conversation. The intention is to suggest that we can become like Adam and Eve in their innocent sexuality, insofar as we can surmount the consequences of the Fall. Milton achieves this by having the first people symbolically replicate the appearance and piety of his contemporary Puritans:

> in their looks divine
> The image of their glorious maker shone,
> Truth, wisdom, sanctitude severe and pure,
> Severe, but in true filial freedom placed;
> Whence true authority in men; though both
> Not equal, as their sex not equal seemed;
> For contemplation he and valour formed,
> For softness she and sweet attractive grace,
> He for God only, she for God in him:

His fair large front and eye sublime declared
Absolute rule; and hyacinthine locks
Round from his parted forelock manly hung
Clustering, but not beneath his shoulders broad:
She as a veil down to the slender waist
Her unadornèd golden tresses wore
Dishevelled, but in wanton ringlets waved
As the vine curls her tendrils, which implied
Subjection, but required with gentle sway,
And by her yielded, by him best received,
Yielded with coy submission, modest pride,
And sweet reluctant amorous delay.

(IV.291–311)

Milton portrays hair to the shoulder but not below for the man and Eve's clothlike tresses figuring the veil worn by primitive Christian and later godly women in church services. All hint of lewdness is supposed to be absent, because we are in a prelapsarian world. Nonetheless, we cannot help thinking about those later fallen associations. This is a crucial part of the poem's duality. Still, Adam and Eve live naked, work as gardeners, and eat as vegetarians, the latter feature replicating the idealism of some of Milton's coreligionists.

The relationship between Adam and Eve turns on the meaning of "one flesh." As Milton gives us his adumbrated version of Genesis, they literally are a somatic continuum, since Eve was formed out of one of Adam's ribs. The text continually makes us feel that sympathy and companionship between the two is a reflex of their material coextension. In Adam's view they are always one continuous being, one flesh; he does not admit of divorce, and Adam and Eve's oneness anticipates the apocalyptic reversal of divorce that will come with the last days. The crunch arrives with the Fall. Where much of the growing difference of opinion between Adam and Eve focuses on the understanding of free will (the subject of Chapter 3), Adam's astonishing speech at the point of his Fall (Eve has already been successfully tempted) involves the fusing of emotions, passions, and flesh that is now familiar, and familiarly vexed:

> How can I live without thee, how forgo
> Thy sweet converse and love so dearly joined,
> To live again in these wild woods forlorn?
> Should God create another Eve, and I
> Another rib afford, yet loss of thee
> Would never from my heart; no no, I feel
> The link of nature draw me: flesh of flesh,
> Bone of my bone thou art, and from thy state
> Mine never shall be parted, bliss or woe.
>
> (IX.908–916)

It may be Latinate syntax, but in English, Adam's sense of loss is signified by a grammatical absence: at line 913, "would never" *what* from his heart? The abrupt caesura that follows and the emotionally disturbed "no, no" underline the point. Some forty lines later, Adam rationalizes his decision:

> I with thee have fixed my lot,
> Certain to undergo like doom, if death
> Consort with thee, death is to me as life;
> So forcible within my heart I feel
> The bond of nature draw me to my own,
> My own in thee, for what thou art is mine;
> Our state cannot be severed, we are one,
> One flesh; to lose thee were to lose my self.

(IX.952–959)

Of course, in choosing to stay with Eve, Adam is divorcing himself from God, and it has been argued that this affirmation of faith in the "bond of nature" (it has been "bond" rather than "link" in these lines), whether it be a psychophysical continuum or merely a bond of affection, is self-deceptive. Adam should really obey the advice of *Tetrachordon,* which was not to lose oneself, and not to lose oneself meant to divorce. The opposition is highly pointed and very deliberate.

Lust is the consequence of the Fall, leading to exhausting sweaty sex ("that fallacious fruit,/That with exhilarating vapour bland/About their spirits had played, and inmost powers/Made err, was now exhaled, and grosser sleep/Bred of unkindly fumes" [IX.1046–

1050]); disgruntled marital relations follow, precisely the state of what has become a flawed marriage as Milton saw it. Adam and Eve wake up into a lifetime of strife, however much their bond of mutual affection fortifies them, and are likened to Samson waking after his fatal haircut "from the harlot-lap of Philistéan Daliláh" (IX.1060–1061). This moment sets up an obvious link with the tortured world of *Samson Agonistes* (1671), where Dalila tries unsuccessfully to pick up the pieces of a wrecked marriage. Silly girl: Samson's outrage is unremitting, to the point of beggaring the verse:

> *Sam.* Out, out hyæna; these are thy wonted arts,
> And arts of every woman false like thee,
> To break all faith, all vows, deceive, betray,
> Then as repentant to submit, beseech,
> And reconcilement move with feigned remorse,
> Confess, and promise wonders in her change,
> Not truly penitent, but chief to try
> Her husband, how far urged his patience bears,
> His virtue or weakness which way to assail:
> Then with more cautious and instructed skill
> Again transgresses, and again submits.
>
> (lines 748–758)

It is an alarming picture of feminine wiles, as Dalila claims that Samson has led her on, that she was only jealous and wanted to keep him because she loved him so much and feared he would run away, she being vulnerable to the persuasions of the Philistian priests. Samson sees this as weakness and as lust; false love, no mutuality. She has broken the law, he says, and has become a prey to false zeal—the idolatry of worshipping the false gods of the Philistines. Her offer to look after the emasculated Samson is met with the opposite response of Adam to Eve at the point of the Fall, but with the same words:

> *Sam.* No, no, of my condition take no care;
> It fits not; thou and I long since are twain;
> Nor think me so unwary or accursed
> To bring my feet again into the snare
> Where once I have been caught; I know thy trains
> Though dearly to my cost.

(lines 928–933)

This is divorce, in the cause of a problematic chosen one, and the male champion is shown often to us as an abused virgin who "gave up my fort of silence to a woman" (line 236), so that the disclosure of the secret of his strength is described as a kind of horrific rape in which Samson is complicit. Even before the Fall, Adam's susceptibility to Eve's presence is sufficient to disorient his ruling reason ("Authority and reason on her wait,/As one intended first, not after made/Occasionally" [VIII.554–556]). Raphael may advise Adam to turn his attention away from "carnal pleasure" and "the sense of touch whereby mankind/Is propagated" (VIII.593, 579–580), but although

Adam tries to look to higher love, he is soon asking Raphael whether the angels touch.

III

In the introduction, I quoted a passage from 1649 in which Milton satirized Charles I's authority by suggesting that he regarded Parliament as if it were subject to his phallic authority: only his presence in it could produce law. In *Paradise Lost,* the creation of the world in Book VII is presented as a gendered process where Mother Earth has within her womb all the objects of creation but nothing will appear until God gives permission. The oceans ferment the hard crust of the earth to produce life, but God has not yet spoken. Then he does:

> The Earth was formed, but in the womb as yet
> Of waters, embryon immature involved,
> Appeared not: over all the face of earth
> Main ocean flowed, not idle, but with warm
> Prolific humour softening all her globe,
> Fermented the great mother to conceive,
> Satiate with genial moisture, when God said
> Be gathered now ye waters under heaven
> Into one place, and let dry land appear.
>
> (VII.276–284)

This is highly charged sexual language, if not exactly erotic. What we are seeing is God's "divorcing" command as divorce or separation is written into the making of objects in the natural world. Since in Milton's heretical universe all matter was originally part of the body of God and God is present in it unless he chooses not to be in it, we are witnessing a description of, so to speak, divine sexuality. The sexual sensuality of the description of creation augurs no less whether mountains or animals are the subject. Fecundity in nature is not to be had without this charged element of description, even if some of the vocabulary has its roots in alchemy or philosophy. This is, as it were, axiomatic sexuality, as opposed to the personal sexuality of Adam and Eve and men and women thereafter. It recalls the sexual imagery of creation at the beginning of Book I, which describes creation as the Holy Spirit's impregnation of Chaos: "thou from the first/Wast present, and with mighty wings outspread/Dovelike satst brooding on the vast abyss/And mad'st it pregnant" (I.19–22). Since Milton held that God created the universe out of himself, rather than out of nothing, *ex nihilo,* the more conventional view, we have to assume that this is a description of a sexual act of one entity with itself. Later, in Book VIII, Milton has Raphael suggest that there might be other worlds, so divided between "the two great sexes" (VIII.151).

In the realm of persons and personality, this cosmology appears to have certain characteristics. Creating/divorcing God is an author, and all the male characters after him in the poem—Satan, Adam, and of course the narrator—are typified by the acts of authorship they understand and exercise. The authority that these three embody is prophetic, including, in a negative sense, that of Satan. The angels are exceptions, since they are so obviously messengers, although Raphael is heavily engaged in the construction of prophetic narratives. The Son is a different matter and is discussed later (see Chapter 4). Eve, Sin, and Mother Earth, on the other hand, are producers. Eve's consciousness is represented very nearly as a byproduct of her fecundity, and as something that ranges beyond the control of male reason or authority. In this respect, the relationship between Adam and Eve is not quite identical to that between the land and the sea, once they are created by the "divorcing command," since they simply belong together. But with Eve, the seeds of what is presented as a mental error and a frailty are sown when her first moment of consciousness is also a moment of self-reflection in the pool:

> Not distant far from thence a murmuring sound
> Of waters issued from a cave and spread
> Into a liquid plain, then stood unmoved
> Pure as the expanse of heaven; I thither went
> With unexperienced thought, and laid me down
> On the green bank, to look into the clear
> Smooth lake, that to me seemed another sky.
> As I bent down to look, just opposite,
> A shape within the watery gleam appeared
> Bending to look on me, I started back,
> It started back, but pleased I soon returned,

> Pleased it returned as soon with answering looks
> Of sympathy and love; there I had fixed
> Mine eyes till now, and pined with vain desire,
> Had not a voice thus warned me, What thou seest,
> What there thou seest fair creature is thyself,
> With thee it came and goes: but follow me,
> And I will bring thee where no shadow stays
> Thy coming, and thy soft embraces, he
> Whose image thou art, him thou shall enjoy
> Inseparably thine, to him shalt bear
> Multitudes like thyself, and thence be called
> Mother of human race.
>
> (IV.453–475)

The question begged by the narrative is, is the guiding voice able to offer sufficient direction, or does the Ovidian, narcissistic moment represent a trajectory of profound difference and dissent within Eden and for humankind: feminine thought? For some readers these lines are an amazing account of same-sex desire before Eve's innocent but amorous impulses are regulated, a waywardness that has to be reclaimed by the heterosexuality of the poem's order, the story of the lesbian's denial at the very birth of her self-consciousness.

The other component in Eve's "rebellion" is labor. Adam and Eve are enjoined by God to work the garden, but it is too large, and "wanton growth" turns tamed nature back to wild. When they are together, they spend far too much time in enjoyment of each other, as opposed to working hard in the garden (IX.220–225). They are promised children, who will help them till the soil, but the subject of the separation scene in Book IX, which leaves Eve open to Satan's temptation, is a dispute over horticultural method. Eve believes that they will work more efficiently if they go separately, whereas Adam is happy for them to sacrifice efficiency on the understanding that they will catch up when children arrive, and after all, the injunction to labor does not in his view override God's intention that humans were made to appreciate delight and reason.

We leave Adam and Eve at the end of *Paradise Lost* very much in a state of fallen mutuality, "hand in hand with wandering steps and slow,/Through Eden took their solitary way" (XII.648–649). We have not witnessed the divorce of Adam and Eve, but, with all the sense of a tragic catharsis behind us, we have witnessed the end of "one flesh," with Satan as putative adulterer. Yet if this union was desirable in some respects, in others the metaphysics of divorce are crucial in explaining how some elements in the world should never cleave to each other:

> If church and state shall be made one flesh again as under the law, let it be withal considered that God, who then joined them, hath now severed them; that which, he so ordaining, was then a lawful conjunction to such on either side as join again what he hath severed would be nothing now but their own presumptuous fornication.
>
> (*A Treatise of Civil Power, CPW,* VII, 261)

3

FREE WILL

In the second edition of *The Doctrine and Discipline of Divorce* (February 1644), Milton stressed that marriage of incompatible partners was a sin. Since God could not be held responsible for sin, divorce must have divine sanction. He illustrated the point by a comparison of this aspect of the divorce argument with the charges made by the Jesuits and the Arminians against the Calvinists: that predestination theology made God responsible for man's sin, since it appeared to argue that human free will was dominated by divine necessity. Milton hinted at a passage in Calvin's *Institutes* underlining prelapsarian Adam's uninhibited exercise of free will (*CPW*, II.293). The followers of the Dutch theologian Jacobus Arminius (1560–1609), who challenged Calvinist theology in the name of postlapsarian man's potential to exercise his own free will, are presented as religious opponents in error. Did Milton do this in order to appeal to as many orthodox

Protestants as possible in the matter of divorce? Or did he really mean it? It is striking that about ten months later, in *Areopagitica* (November 1644), Milton published a view of theology that was the opposite, which is to say Arminian:

> Many there be that complain of divine Providence for suffering *Adam* to transgress, foolish tongues! When God gave him reason, he gave him freedom to choose, for reason is but choosing; he had been else a mere artificial Adam, such an Adam as he is in the motions. We ourselves esteem not of that obedience, or love, or gift, which is of force: God therefore left him free, set before him a provoking object, ever almost in his eyes; herein consisted his merit, herein the right of his reward, the praise of his abstinence. Wherefore did he create passions within us, pleasures round about us, but that these rightly tempered are the very ingredients of virtue?
>
> (*Areopagitica, CPW,* II.527)

The difference between Adam and post-Fall man has been eradicated in *Areopagitica:* we all have the power to exercise free will, and in so doing choose good over evil or not. Even then, Milton still states that Arminius was "perverted" by the books he read (*CPW,* II.519–520) while offering an Arminian theology.

This position is set out with schoolmasterly clarity near the beginning of Book III of *Paradise Lost* as God foretells the Fall of man:

> I made him just and right,
> Sufficient to have stood, though free to fall.

> Such I created all the ethereal powers
> And spirits, both them who stood and them who failed;
> Freely they stood who stood, and fell who fell.
> Not free, what proof could they have given sincere
> Of true allegiance, constant faith or love?
> Where only what they needs must do, appeared,
> Not what they would, what praise could they receive?
> What pleasure I from such obedience paid,
> When will and reason (reason also is choice)
> Useless and vain, of freedom both despoiled,
> Made passive both, had served necessity,
> Not me.

(III.98–111)

This is certainly not expressed with the optimism of *Areopagitica*, but it is in Milton's understanding that the Son's atonement buys fallen mankind the chance to exercise his or her own free will. The Son makes the point again in Book X.77–79. In *De Doctrina Christiana* (1655–), this assumption is clear; fallen man has free will:

> We imagine nothing unworthy of God if we maintain that those results, those conditions which God himself has chosen to place within man's free power, depend upon man's free will. In fact, God made his decrees conditional in this way for the very purpose of allowing free causes to put into effect that freedom which he himself gave them.

(*CPW*, VI.160)

As Milton says later on, in *A Treatise of Civil Power in Ecclesiastical Causes* (1659), "The will not free, becomes no will" (*CPW,* VII.256). And in order to push the point home in *Paradise Lost,* Milton explicitly exempts God's foreknowledge (he does not mention predestination) from having any impact on the Fall, howsoever he foreknew it:

> they themselves decreed
> Their own revolt, not I: if I foreknew,
> Foreknowledge had no influence on their fault,
> Which had no less proved certain unforeknown.
> So without least impulse or shadow of fate,
> Or aught by me immutably foreseen,
> They trespass, authors to themselves in all
> Both what they judge and what they choose; for so
> I formed them free, and free they must remain,
> Till they enthrall themselves.
>
> (III.116–125)

It is Raphael's task, says God in Book V, to tell Adam of this faculty and of the need to guard it:

> such discourse bring on,
> As may advise him of his happy state,
> Happiness in his power left free to will,
> Left to his own free will, his will though free,
> Yet mutable; whence warn him to beware

> He swerve not too secure: tell him withal
> His danger, and from whom.

(V.233–239)

"Reason also is choice" (*Paradise Lost,* III.108) echoes the earlier phrase in *Areopagitica,* "reason is but choosing," which itself repeats a phrase from the slightly earlier *Of Education* (5 June 1644): "By this time, years and good general precepts will have furnished them more distinctly with that act of reason which in *Ethics* is called *Proairesis:* that they may with some judgment contemplate upon moral good and evil" (*CPW,* II.396). προαίρεσις *(proairesis)* means "choice," and is used by Aristotle in his *Nicomachean Ethics,* II.vi.15, to define moral virtue. There are two points of interest here. One is the sense that Milton seems to be putting a Greek philosophical formulation into the heart of Christian theology. Indeed, since man's free will is the image of God in him, God has become, as it were, Aristotle—not a matter of small import, although it is also the case that Milton found the concept in the patristic writers Tertullian and Lactantius and noted it as such in the Commonplace Book:

> In moral evil much good can be mixed and that with remarkable cunning: "No one combines poison with gall, and with hellebore, but with savory sauces and delicacies . . . So the devil steeps whatever deadly dish he prepares in God's dearest . . . benefits," &c. Tertull: de spectaculis p[age] 102 edit. Rigalt:
>   Why does God permit evil? . . . As Lactantius says, Book 5.

c[hapter] 7, that reason and intelligence may have the opportunity to exercise themselves by choosing the things that are good, by fleeing from the things that are evil. Lactan de ira dei. C[hapter] 13.

(*CPW*, I.362–363)

Second, we can see in *proairesis* the word "heresy." Milton insists that heresy is not that which is defined by the church or a church as abhorrent to official teaching, but that which is arrived at by choice through reason, because that is originally what heresy means: choice. It is a small step to seeing that choosing with the power of reason means we must have a relatively tolerant society.

The classical configurations of choosing are never far from Milton's attention. In *The Doctrine and Discipline of Divorce*, Adam and Eve (or rather free will), as we discover, map onto Epithemus and Pandora, even though it was the male Epithemus who chose to open Pandora's box,[1] whereas it is Eve herself who is tempted. Milton also finds proof in Homer and in the cosmological Roman poet Manilius that human will, in addition to Fate, is responsible for man's woes.[2] This is a more recognizable Renaissance fusion of Judeo-Christian and Greco-Roman systems, but recourse to the tracts of the 1640s reveals the extent of Milton's immersion in classical civic thought as he constructed his ideas of free will and heresy. *Of Education* presents a view of vigorous civic virtue practiced through rigorous training and strict morals. It is militaristic in part, and while it does not ignore theology, the ambit is decidedly worldly: "I call therefore a complete and generous education that which fits a man to perform justly, skillfully and magnanimously all the offices both private and public of peace and war" (*Of Education, CPW,* II, 377–379). More directly, "the main skill and groundwork will be, to temper them such lectures and explanations upon every opportunity, as may lead and draw them in willing obedience, enflamed with the study of learning, and the admiration of virtue; stirred up with high hopes of living to be brave men, and worthy patriots, dear to God, and famous to all ages" (II, 384–385).

This vision finds its fulfillment in *Areopagitica*'s picture of a vibrant London full of writers, all of whom are seeking to find the truth. Militarism is matched with a kind of vitalism:

> For books are not absolutely dead things, but doe contain a potency of life in them to be as active as that soul was whose progeny they are; nay they do preserve as in a viol the purest efficacy and extraction of that living intellect that bred them. I know they are as lively, and as vigorously productive, as those fabulous dragon's teeth; and being sown up and down, may chance to spring up armed men. And yet on the other hand, unless wariness be used, as good almost kill a man as kill a good book; who kills a man kills a reasonable creature, God's image; but he who destroys a good book, kills reason it self, kills the image of God, as it were in the eye.
>
> (*Areopagitica, CPW,* II.492)

The public exposure of different published viewpoints, through debate and printed response, will, Milton opines, result in a collective establishment of the truth. Writers make (hopefully virtuous) choices between good and evil, and so do readers. That's why men have free will, and why there should be little censorship.

Much has been written of the contradictions or shortcomings of *Areopagitica:* that Milton never extends toleration to Roman Catholics (because he argued they threatened to incite violent resistance to English governments) and argues that blasphemous books should in fact be burned. These are but two of a larger series of paradoxes that pass through the core of *Areopagitica,* perhaps almost deliberately, so that each reader has to make the choice between good and evil at the level of an apprehension of the very structure, or should I say chaotically various energy, of the tract.

Writing itself is seen as reproduction, and censorship would be like plugging a womb: "No envious *Juno* sat cross-legged over the nativity of any mans intellectual offspring; but if it proved a monster, who denies, but that it was justly burned, or sunk into the sea" (*Areopagitica, CPW,* II.505). Literary life is inherently to do with choosing rightly. There is a famous misreading of Spenser, where Milton has the Palmer follow Guyon in the Cave of Mammon. Spenser's point is that the well-balanced man does not need holiness to help him resist the temptation to worldly greed and so the Palmer does not enter the cave. Milton's misreading suggests that divinity and human reason are fused in one mental presence. There are also some perplexing fusions of opposite positions on grace, antinomianism (the belief that one is so certain of grace that one cannot sin) appearing with the scripture that to the pure all things are pure but sitting directly before a sentence that claims the opposite. We have to choose what we eat, goes Milton's figure, but he hopes that at least bad books will be a warning to good men. It is not an economy of knowledge that is consistently defined but rather one that lurches from instances where control over publishing and expression is described to one that attempts to capture emblematically the idea of reading and writing as an endless separation of good from evil:

> Good and evil we know in the field of this world grow up together almost inseparably; and the knowledge of good is so involved and interwoven with the knowledge of evil, and in so many cunning resemblances hardly to be discerned, that those confused seeds which were imposed on *Psyche* as an incessant labour to cull out, and sort asunder, were not more intermixed. It was from out the rind of one apple tasted, that the knowledge of good and evil as two twins cleaving together leapt forth into the world. And perhaps this is that doom which *Adam* fell into of knowing good and evil, that is to say of knowing good by evil.

> (*Areopagitica, CPW,* II.514)

And this is by way of preface to one of the most influential statements in all of Milton, envisioning life as a purifying trial in which endless, successive virtuous choices must be achieved:

He that can apprehend and consider vice with all her baits and seeming pleasures, and yet abstain, and yet distinguish, and yet prefer that which is truly better, he is the true wayfaring Christian. I cannot praise a fugitive and cloistered virtue, unexercised and unbreathed, that never sallies out and sees her adversary, but slinks out of the race, where that immortal garland is to be run for, not without dust and heat. Assuredly we bring not innocence into the world, we bring impurity much rather: that which purifies us is trial, and trial is by what is contrary.

(Areopagitica, CPW, II.514–515)

But the contrary is not just a binary choice between good and evil. Contrariness, which is both explained by Milton and suggested time and again by his imagery, is the condition created by recent developments in the means of communication, print in particular. Once published and circulated, books cannot be entirely silenced; suppression at home will not stop foreign production of books and their surreptitious circulation at home; indeed, suppression may well aid the suppressed book as it gains cachet. The work of the licensers is in fact impossible, and what would be done for books that are partly good and partly bad? The confusing expurgations attempted by the Inquisition? The most interesting image that Milton uses here is of a dung heap that grows inexorably even as people try to clear it away:

They are not skilful considerers of human things, who imagine to remove sin by removing the matter of sin; for, besides that it is a huge heap increasing under the very act of diminishing, though some part of it may for a time be withdrawn from some persons, it cannot from all, in such a universal thing as books are; and when this is done, yet the sin remains entire.

(Areopagitica, CPW, II.527)

By now, of course, Milton has long left behind the narrow remit of licensing and is talking about moral and ethical behavior in more general terms.

What Milton is addressing, what he calls the condition of "philosophic freedom," is an imagined public sphere in which free will underwrites a capitalism of ideas, where individuals (and Milton meant educated ones) are dedicated to the discovery of the highest merchandise, "Truth":

Truth and understanding are not such wares as to be monopolized and traded in by tickets and statutes, and standards. We must not think to make a staple commodity of all the knowledge in the land, to mark and license it like our broad cloth, and our wool packs. What is it but a servitude like that imposed by the Philistines, not to be allowed the sharpening of our own axes and coulters, but we must repair from all quarters to twenty licensing forges.

(Areopagitica, CPW, II.535–536)

The gathering of truth is not therefore to be regulated by licensers as if it were either a commodity subject to restrictive monopolies or an antiquated guild structure. Neither must it be alienated by paying someone else to gather it or look after it for you; it is radically identified with and internalized in the subject. Knowledge is a search where the customary is always being challenged and overturned in a perpetual intellectual muscularity. There is a degree of aggression here that anticipates Satan's character: Milton is relishing the chance to controvert timid ministers who hide behind the orthodoxy of the licensers (as indeed some 1640s divines expressed fear of having to controvert Milton). Milton's definition of truth as a supercommodity looks a long way forward into history, not merely to the era of free trade (which he and some of his contemporaries were advocating in the 1640s) but to our own world, in which information itself has become a valuable commodity in a globe tied together by information technology.

Areopagitica's greatest influence was not to come in Milton's lifetime, and perhaps its impact is still to peak. In his own time, the tract's ideas were seen to soar above the needs of religious, scientific, and educational reformers, and the center of republican theorizing was not in this area. Yet we must acknowledge and appreciate this farsightedness. Milton characterizes intellectual labor, and we might say that Western governments ever since have been trying to harness this vision of enormous potential both to a harmonious, stable, and just social order and to one where the maximum benefit of this energy is yielded:

> Behold now this vast city: a city of refuge, the mansion house of liberty, encompassed and surrounded with his protection; the shop of war hath not there more anvils and hammers waking, to fashion out the plates and instruments of armed Justice in defense of beleaguered Truth, then there be pens and heads there, sitting by their studious lamps, musing, searching, revolving new notions and ideas wherewith to present, as with their homage and their fealty the approaching Reformation: others as fast reading, trying all things, assenting to the force of reason and convincement. What could a man require more from a nation so pliant and so prone to seek after knowledge.
>
> (*Areopagitica, CPW,* II.553–554)

To do otherwise is to freeze society in a way that God never intended: "There have been not a few since the beginning of this Parliament, both of the Presbytery and others who by their unlicensed books to the contempt of an *Imprimatur* first broke that triple ice clung about our hearts, and taught the people to see day" (*Areopagitica, CPW,* II.568).

All this daring and exhilarating argument suggests Satan. Satan's language in Book II of *Paradise Lost* is distinctly that of free will, right, and merit. The latter two terms belong in the next two chapters' discussions of political terms. The first point to note is that Satan does not know, or has lost the ability to understand, the theological universe in which he exists. Thus it is God who prescribes his lot in stark terms at the beginning of Book III. Satan believes his defeat is a consequence of fate, but God knows he rules the universe. In terms of dramatic, classical, and theological tradition, Satan is a tragic hero in a voluntarist universe. "Just right" is his first explanation for his wicked eminence as leader of the angelic rebellion, but the second cause is "free choice," which in a sense is true—Satan has chosen to fall (II.18–24). The fallen angels "complain that fate/Free virtue should enthral to force or chance" (II.550–551), but this is ancient *virtus,* manliness, not choice. Nonetheless, other fallen angels discuss "providence, foreknowledge, will and fate,/Fixt fate, free will, foreknowledge absolute" (II.559–560) but cannot conclude; they cheer themselves up with false surmises and in general are lost, sliding first in the absence of scriptural authority to mere scholastic debate (as chastised in *Areopagitica*) and then to Stoic philosophy, "Vain wisdom all, and false philosophy" (II.565), which the Son will deride in Book IV of *Paradise Regained.* In *Paradise Lost,* Book V, Raphael explains to Adam and Eve how it is for angels and men:

> Our voluntary service he requires,
> Not our necessitated, such with him
> Finds no acceptance, nor can find, for how
> Can hearts, not free, be tried whether they serve
> Willing or no, who will but what they must
> By destiny, and can no other choose?
>
> (V.529–534)

Free will makes full sense when it is conjunct with obedience: "freely we serve/Because we freely love, as in our will/To love or not; in this we stand or fall" (V.538–540). It is a hard thing to achieve.

Now Satan is a jealous guy, and his rebellion is rooted in envy of the honors that God gives to the Son. The rebellion is expressed again in political terms, but Satan also works through classical ethical values that have become corrupted. In ancient republicanism, envy should be converted to emulation, the desire to excel those with whom one competes—a sense that is more in keeping with the vibrant energy of the militant truth-seekers in *Areopagitica*. The characters in the poem who certainly contemplate free will are Adam and Eve, and it is in the separation scene in Book IX that Milton dramatizes two sides of the debate that do not quite emerge in *Areopagitica*. The scene has been convincingly regarded as a reflection of the difference between antinomianism (Eve) and an Arminianism well regulated by an ultimate faith in God, positions that, as we have seen, are actually mixed up in *Areopagitica*. Of course, before the Fall, these theological positions do not exist, but they are figured in the debate. It is when Eve explains her faith in God's support, that he surely would not subject them to temptation without some kind of guard, that our attention should be triggered: "And what is faith, love, virtue unassayed/Alone, without exterior help sustained?" (IX.335–336). It seems a good argument, but Adam is more cautious:

> God left free the will, for what obeys
> Reason, is free, and reason he made right,
> But bid her well beware, and still erect,

> Lest by some fair appearing good surprised
> She dictate false, and misinform the will
> To do what God expressly hath forbid,
> Not then mistrust, but tender love enjoins,
> That I should mind thee oft, and mind thou me.
> Firm we subsist, yet possible to swerve,
> Since reason not impossibly may meet
> Some specious object by the foe suborned,
> And fall into deception unaware,
> Not keeping strictest watch.

(IX.351–363)

Adam introduces the concept of "right reason" here: the power to choose but also one that always puts obedience to God first and foremost. Satan is the first to alienate right reason. But Adam is caught, since he cannot compel Eve to stay: that would be a compromise of her innocence. So he must let her go to face the trial that we've already heard about in *Areopagitica:*

> But if thou think, trial unsought may find
> Us both securer then thus warned thou seemst,
> Go; for thy stay, not free, absents thee more;
> Go in thy native innocence, rely
> On what thou hast of virtue, summon all,
> For God towards thee hath done his part, do thine.

(IX.370–375)

The whole poem, and Milton's view of the history of mankind, turns on these lines, and they have been much discussed in terms of whether Eve was presumptuous or Adam insufficiently responsible in not restraining her. But leaving the choice so balanced deliberately conveys the dilemma in the theological issue, and the only crucial difference between God and Adam at this point is that Adam does not have foreknowledge. Of course, if only he did.

It is worth considering the different kinds of argument attributed to Adam and Eve here. Eve is recognizably antinomian, and her mode of piety distinctly resembles the reliance on dreams and visions that typified the religious radicals of Milton's day, and especially the women who were prominent in those congregations. After she has eaten the apple, Eve claims that her own "experience" (IX.807) is her best guide after the Tree of the Knowledge of Good and Evil. This brings to mind the theology of "experience" or "experimental theology," the application of syllogistic reasoning to one's memory of experience in order to understand how God is working on one, which predominated in the sects, and especially among the Independents, Puritans who believed in self-gathering and self-governing congregation; a confession of faith and of experience was a requirement of membership. It was a major element in the spiritual autobiography or conversion narrative of Milton's time. Eve is seduced by Satan in a dream and given an impression of power through flight—precisely the kind of dream that occurs in the published collections of conversion narratives. Such is Satan's triumph; Eve merely mimics him after the Fall, doing poor service to the value of experience. Indeed, her appeal to the reliability of experience is precisely the opposite, for she is utterly misguided. Is not Milton associating Eve with (female) radical Puritan piety and castigating it? After all, by 1667 it could be said that experience had not served the Puritans well at all. Although he is correctly seen as a fellow traveler of so many radical Puritans, Milton left no conversion narrative and is not known to have been a member of any particular congregation. Indeed, the linguistic material that recorded and helped him understand his own piety, in addition to the Bible, was the classical and European literary tradition. His "conversion narrative" in consequence looks a whole lot more courtly, if not clerical. However Milton praised and defended the sects in the closing pages of *Areopagitica*, and however he left reassuring messages for them in *Paradise Regained*, there is undoubted gender prejudice here with regard to feminine piety, one that has been seen as inevitable given the time and context in which Milton lived. Perhaps he was not so delighted to learn, in the pages of his Presbyterian persecutor, Thomas Edwards, of the Mrs. Attaway who held up a copy of *The Doctrine and Discipline of Divorce* in her conventicle's meetings, using it to justify separation from her ungodly husband.

If you are fallen, you lose your reason, and that's what happens to Adam and Eve, as is evident in their fallacious reasoning immediately after the Fall, the well-documented puns, and the remorseful bickering. Free will is also a somewhat better thing in an unfallen world; after the Fall it is compromised by mortality, the smell of which delights Death (X.272–281). Eve's suggestion that she and Adam commit suicide is a final beggary of free will (X.1001–1006).

Free will is intimately related knowledge, and knowledge is a food. The proximity of nutrition for the body and for the mind (and for Milton there can ultimately be no difference between the two) is made evident in *Areopagitica:*

> For books are as meats and viands are; some of good, some of evil substance; and yet God in that unapocryphal vision, said without exception, Rise *Peter,* kill and eat, leaving the choice to each man's discretion. Wholesome meats to a vitiated stomach differ little or nothing from unwholesome; and best books to a naughty mind are not unappliable to occasions of evil. Bad meats will scarce breed good nourishment in the healthiest concoction; but herein the difference is of bad books, that they to a discreet and judicious reader serve in many respects to discover, to confute, to forewarn, and to illustrate.
>
> (*CPW,* II.512–513)

The conjunction is explored delightfully at the center of *Paradise Lost,* as Raphael explains the way the universe works to Adam. Angels, it would seem, eat knowledge, and Raphael has a matter converter, so that he can derive nourishment from earthly food:

what he gives

> (Whose praise be ever sung) to man in part
> Spiritual, may of purest spirits be found
> No ingrateful food: and food alike those pure
> Intelligential substances require
> As doth your rational; and both contain
> Within them every lower faculty
> Of sense, whereby they hear, see, smell, touch, taste,
> Tasting concoct, digest, assimilate,
> And corporeal to incorporeal turn.

(V.404–413)

The expression again implies dualism, but in fact the system of nourishment must be based on the continuity of all matter in creation—it is simply more or less refined, as we have seen. When Eve serves salad-bar supper, we learn a new definition of a key theological term. "Transubstantiation" is no longer the transformation of the host into the body and blood of Christ but the transformation of matter to spirit by ordinary suggestion, which by the way suggests that Adam and Eve before the Fall enjoy communion with God and the divine beings:

> So down they sat,
> And to their viands fell, nor seemingly
> The Angel, nor in mist, the common gloss

Of theologians, but with keen dispatch
Of real hunger, and concoctive heat
To transubstantiate; what redounds, transpires
Through spirits with ease; nor wonder; if by fire
Of sooty coal the empiric alchemist
Can turn, or holds it possible to turn
Metals of drossiest ore to perfect gold
As from the mine.

(V.433–443)

Soon comes the promise we've all been waiting for, and that which is promised by communion/eating as Milton defines it:

Wonder not then, what God for you saw good
If I refuse not, but convert, as you,
To proper substance; time may come when men
With angels may participate, and find
No inconvenient diet, nor too light fare:
And from these corporal nutriments perhaps
Your bodies may at last turn all to spirit,
Improved by tract of time, and winged ascend
Ethereal, as we, or may at choice
Here or in heavenly paradises dwell.

(V.491–500)

So much for an open choice of menu. Back in the postlapsarian world, it falls to Samson to express that sense in very late Milton that upholds free-will theology as we have seen it since *Areopagitica,* but here it is hedged about (since Samson does not know about Jesus) by an utter uncertainty over the future and the real possibility that despite free will, one may still incur God's wrath:

> If I obey them,
> I do it freely; venturing to displease
> God for the fear of man, and man prefer,
> Set God behind: which in his jealousy
> Shall never, unrepented, find forgiveness.
> Yet that he may dispense with me or thee
> Present in temples at idolatrous rites
> For some important cause, thou need'st not doubt.
>
> (lines 1372–1379)

4

TYRANNY AND KINGSHIP

I

Between the publication of the 1645 *Poems* on 2 January 1646 (in old-style dating, the year didn't change until March 25) and the appearance of *The Tenure of Kings and Magistrates* on 13 February 1649, Milton published nothing, and he disappeared from view as an active controversialist and poet. A lot can happen in three years. There was much to deal with in his private life in this time—his father died in January 1647, leaving him with a house in Bread Street, London, and an income to organize, and he sought to obtain further property in Oxfordshire as a belated part of his wife's dowry (Mary Powell having returned to his house in 1645). His nephew and pupil Edward Phillips says that Milton moved to a smaller house in High Holborn, backing onto Lincoln's Inn Fields, and continued to read books intensely.

In the meantime, a great deal happened in church and state. Parliament decisively won the civil war and tried to reach a settlement with the king. A Presbyterian *Directory of Public Worship* was issued, but the Independents, the Baptists, and other Puritan religious groups to the left of the Presbyterians began to flex their muscles. In Milton's London, religious difference was the order of the day, and there and in the New Model Army, the Levellers demanded greater religious toleration and populist constitutional reform. A settlement with the king was not reached, and a further royalist uprising precipitated the brief second civil war in the summer of 1648. The king was brought to trial and executed in January 1649—for the great majority, a wholly unexpected event.

We have to assume that Milton was listening to and watching public life through these traumatic years. The grounds for doing so are evident in *The Tenure of Kings and Magistrates,* which reveals his serious engagement in the matter of what makes a king turn into a tyrant and the grounds upon which such a ruler might be removed. Milton was familiar with republican writing long before this point; there are references to Machiavelli, for instance, in the Commonplace Book that go back to the early 1640s, although in the anti-episcopal tracts he could still entertain the notion of a godly king, unhindered by corrupt bishops. Yet he followed the issue initially not in republican theory but in the feudal law of the king's power, a debate that became increasingly urgent as the 1640s wore on. The closer the removal of the king came, the more vital the issue of defending Parliament's right to resist became. *The Tenure of Kings and Magistrates* is a full-scale investigation of the English monarchy in biblical, classical, and European terms. In it emerged for the first time Milton's anti-tyrannical aesthetics, a shocking onslaught, in the name of godly iconoclasm, on all forms of oppressive authority. It embraces justified violence and in a very precise way launches an offensive on the literary tradition that had sustained the writer in his developing years. If the mid-1640s tracts generated a vision of exciting variety as truth was debated and discovered through contradiction, now singular destructiveness became a principle. However awesome, this vision is also in places abhorrent. We have to confront the fact that Milton had a violent imagination, or was at least prepared to countenance the presence of violence as part of his creativity.

Milton's attack on tyranny begins where the divorce tracts end: "But being slaves within doors, no wonder that they strive so much to have the public state conformably governed to the inward vicious rule, by which they govern themselves . . . Some contesting for privileges, customs, forms, and that old entanglement of iniquity, their gibberish laws, though the badge of their ancient slavery" (*The Tenure, CPW,* III.190, 192–193). Milton is attacking the Presbyterians, because for all their initial support for the civil war, they did not want to put the king on trial and see him executed. The problem with the Presbyterians, says Milton, was that they were simply lost to an old way of seeing, "a carnal admiring of that worldly pomp and greatness" (*The Tenure, CPW,* III.193). Slavery induces cowardly behavior, as Milton later reminded one of his opponents in the 1650s who chose to publish anonymously (*The Tenure, CPW,* IV.i.561).

In this political context, contrariness is described not as a positive habit of mind, as in *Areopagitica,* but as its opposite: an outward behavior and a condition of Presbyterian deceit with "cloven tongues of falsehood and dissention." Furthermore,

> nor let any man be deluded by either the ignorance or the notorious hypocrisy and self-repugnance of our dancing divines, who have the conscience and the boldness, to come with Scripture in their mouths, glossed and fitted for their turns with a double contradictory sense, transforming the sacred verity of God, to an idol with two faces, looking at once two several ways; and with the same quotations to charge others, which in the same case they made serve to justify themselves.
>
> (*The Tenure, CPW,* III.195–196)

Ancient views of the likelihood of monarchy to degenerate into tyranny are also present. Milton would soon be prominent as one of the most convinced classical republicans, foregrounding the reclaimed teachings of Greek tragedy and history:

> How much more rationally spake the heathen king *Demophoon* in a tragedy of Euripides then these interpreters would put upon King *David,* "I rule not my people by tyranny, as if they were barbarians,

but am my self liable, if I do unjustly, to suffer justly." Not unlike was the speech of *Trajan* the worthy emperor, to one whom he made general of his Praetorian forces. "Take this drawn sword", saith he, "to use for me, if I reign well, if not, to use against me." Thus *Dion* relates.

(The Tenure, CPW, III.205–206)

The *Greeks* and *Romans,* as their prime authors witness, held it not only lawful, but a glorious and heroic deed, rewarded publicly with statues and garlands, to kill an infamous tyrant at any time without trial: and but reason, that he who trod down all law, should not be vouchsafed the benefit of law. Insomuch that *Seneca* the tragedian brings in *Hercules* the grand suppressor of tyrants, thus speaking,

> ——————*Victima haud ulla amplior*
> *Potest, magisque opima mactari Jovi*
> *Quam Rex iniquus*——————-
>
> ——————*There can be slaine*
> *No sacrifice to God more acceptable*
> *Then an unjust and wicked King*——————

(The Tenure, CPW, III.212–213)

Charles I's disrespect for his people marks his tyranny: "So many beasts, or vermin under his feet, not to be reasoned with, but to be trod on; among whom there might be found so many thousand men for wisdom, vertue, nobleness of mind" (*The Tenure, CPW,* III.204–205). When the crimes of a tyrant are evident, as Milton felt they manifestly were in the case of Charles I, this kind of fierce and absolute heroic writing is justified, and connected with the citation of authorities calling for the removal of bad kings or insisting that monarchies be elected rather than hereditary, so that a defective king may more readily be subject to replacement. But the argument is nonetheless chilling. It appeared to the king's supporters as an act of illegal or even devilish redefinition.

Milton's polemic against monarchs exhibits renaming as high art, and this tendency is exaggerated in *Eikonoklastes* (October 1649), Milton's attack on Charles I's posthumously published defense of himself (in fact cowritten by the king and several of his advisers), *Eikon Basilike*, partly because Milton was consciously engaging in an act of Protestant image-breaking. The writing necessarily embodies a kind of affective violence.

Eikonoklastes is huge (227 quarto pages), not least because it takes on *Eikon Basilike* page by page. Several sections are notably inventive, as Milton plays with the king's image to suggest that a monarch is at his best, at his liveliest, when he is dead: "And how much their intent, who published these overlate apologies and meditations of the dead King, drives to the same end of stirring up the people to bring him that honour, that affection, and by consequence, that revenge to his dead corps, which he himself living could never gain to his person" (*Eikonoklastes, CPW*, III.342). A related perception of decayed vastness had already been voiced in *The Tenure* ("the mere useless bulk of his person" [*CPW*, III.197]), which perhaps also connects with the huge body of Satan lying on the burning lake in *Paradise Lost*, Book I. The iconoclasm works by an invocation of literary tradition, apt enough since Milton saw that *Eikon Basilike* was a poem: "The words are good, the fiction smooth and cleanly; there wanted only rhyme" (*Eikonoklastes, CPW*, III.406). In the preface, the famous woodcut engraving of Charles had seemed a "masking scene," "set there to catch fools and silly gazers." Tyranny has been turned into art. The grand statement of the English Protestant literary tradition, Spenser's *The Faerie Queene*, becomes for Milton the reservoir in which righteous violence, be it legislative or actual, is enacted. Thus Spenser's Talus, Artegall's iron page and Terminator in Book V, becomes the emblem of the Parliament's work: "I say God send it down, whether by one *Talus*, or by a thousand." On the next page, Talus's iron flail becomes the people themselves (*Eikonoklastes, CPW*, III.390–391). Furthermore, the courtly literature beloved of the Caroline court has led to corruption and idolatry. Charles used Pamela's prayer to Musidorus from Sir Philip Sidney's *Arcadia*, substituting his own voice for Pamela's, God's for Musidorus's. Not that the *Arcadia* is without "worth and wit," but it is scandalously used for the wrong occasion; to steal a prayer from any romance (or anywhere else) is to violate the godly principle that prayer should come spontaneously from the believer's heart.

Yet Milton's attack on Charles's love of Shakespeare is an even more serious charge against Shakespeare himself. The argument begins by showing how tyrants can incorporate pious literature deceitfully into their speeches. Milton knows how much Charles loved Shakespeare and adduces that he learned tyrannous ways from characters like Shakespeare's Richard III, speaking in "as high a strain of piety, and mortification" (*Eikonoklastes, CPW,* III.361). Milton forgets the context of Shakespeare's critical portrayal of Richard and then accuses Shakespeare of distorting history. In fact, Shakespeare's critique of Richard III is not far from Milton's assertion in the *Pro Populo Anglicano Defensio* (first ed. 1651): "For a tyrant, just like a player king indeed, being only a ghost and mask of a king, is not a true king" (56). The sentence in *Eikonoklastes* reads: "The poet used not much license in departing from the truth of history, which delivers him a deep dissembler, not of his affections only, but of religion" (*CPW,* III.362). Shakespeare helps Milton to discover Charles I's tyranny, but did Milton think that a knowledge of Shakespeare would encourage the king to be tyrannical? Given that the Presbyterians in *The Tenure* are accused of delay in phrasing borrowed from Shakespeare's hostile portrayal of the witches and Lady Macbeth in *Macbeth,* it is clear that Milton's rereading of English and Scottish history at this time involved a critical reappraisal of Shakespearean drama, where the love of Shakespearean language becomes part of a negative world of idolatrous worship, bondage to custom, and slavery to tyrants.[1] In this dark world, Milton's favorite English dramatist, the "native warbler" of "L'Allegro," or at least his works, participate in the font of evil.

Milton thought, against Puritan fashion, that the theaters should be opened, and he was interested in the role of theater during a revolution. There is evidence that he was working on a play between 1647 and 1653, and there have been suspicions that an earlier, now lost version of *Samson Agonistes* is what he wrote (if, on the evidence of *The Tenure*, it was not a revised version of *Macbeth*). If this was the case, then Milton's play participates not merely in the context in which it is customarily placed, the restoration of the monarchy and the revived theater, with its salacious comedies. It also offers a purging of Shakespeare from an inherently neoclassical play (Manoa is Polonius, Dalila Cleopatra, and Harapha a braggart warrior like Othello, and all of them are verbally commanded from the stage by Samson) and a tumultuous act of resistance to tyranny that comes at lines 1649–1650:

> straining all his nerves he bowed,
> As with the force of winds and waters pent,
> When mountains tremble, those two massy pillars
> With horrible convulsion to and fro,
> He tugged, he shook, till down they came and drew
> The whole roof after them, with burst of thunder
> Upon the heads of all who sat beneath,
> Lords, ladies, captains, councillors, or priests,
> Their choice nobility and flower, not only
> Of this but each Philistian city round

Met from all parts to solemnize this feast.
Samson with these immixed, inevitably
Pulled down the same destruction on himself;
The vulgar only scaped who stood without.

(lines 1646–1659)

In other key tracts, Milton worked hard to prove that kings were at worst unnatural and at best only to be appointed by the people. This is the case with *Pro Populo Anglicano Defensio,* Milton's most famous work in Europe, this time defending the regicide against an influential attack by the French classicist Claude de Saumaise, *Defensio Regia* (November 1649). Milton emphatically denies the pervasive argument of the royalists that kings are fathers and breaks this popular analogy by asserting that it is the people who create the king in the first place. He also denies that any monarchy in history has been established by divine right, which has in fact always been an illusion; it was only by God's will that David was exonerated for tyrannous behavior, and it was as a punishment that God gave the Israelites a king (*Pro Populo Anglicano Defensio,* MDz., 92, 95, 97–98).[2] In any case, any father who became a tyrant, for instance by killing his children, would also be punishable under the law. Customary assumptions to the contrary violate the order of nature; worse than a bad political marriage, they are a kind of incest:

And if it hath been anciently interpreted the presaging sign of a future tyrant, but to dream of copulation with his mother, what can it be less then actual tyranny to affirm waking, that the Parliament, which is his mother, can neither conceive or bring forth any authoritative act without his masculine coition: nay that his reason is as celestial and life-giving to the Parliament, as the sun's influence is to the earth: what other notions but these, or such like, could swell up *Caligula* to think himself a god.

(Eikonoklastes, CPW, III.467)

Pro Populo Anglicano Defensio cites a similar example in the story of Antoninus Caracalla and his mother, Julia (MDz., 79). Kings cannot be regarded as above the law, as if this were part of the right of kings, for then the category of tyranny would be entirely annihilated and the royalists would be justified.

II

These energies of definition, denial, and demonization are put to work in *Paradise Lost,* where the fallen angels articulate their predicament through well-known Shakespearean tragic language. The fallen angels speak the language of fallen kings. Thus King Lear's famous heath speech ("You cataracts and hurricanoes, spout," 3.2.2) is combined with an echo of the Vulgate Bible's *cataractae* in Belial's "what if all/Her stores were opened, and this firmament/Of hell should spout her cataracts of fire,/Impendent horrors, threatening hideous fall/One day upon our heads" (II.174–178). The fallen angels believe they have fought a just war against a tyrant, just as Milton accuses his opponent Saumaise of claiming that God is a tyrant (*Pro Populo Anglicano Defensio*, MDz., 99). The predominant angels are infected with the characters of fallen kings from tragedies and English history plays.

Satan, mentioned in *Pro Populo Anglicano Defensio* as the most authoritarian and ruthless kind of despot, appears at the start of Book II as an oriental tyrant: "High on a throne of royal state, which far/Outshone the wealth of Ormus and of Ind,/Or where the gorgeous East with richest hand/Showers on her kings barbaric pearl and gold,/Satan exalted sat" (II.1–5). Confusingly, Satan's discourse embodies free will and republican vocabulary, but it is also the case that he believes he has achieved a kind of restoration of monarchy in hell, without the taint of envy or the strife of faction, since there is no good for which to compete. "We now return/To claim our just inheritance of old,/Surer to prosper then prosperity/Could have assured us" (II.37–40). Later on, when the war in heaven is narrated in Book VI, Raphael claims that Satan's aim in his rebellion was to be placed on God's throne, as a new monarch, so to speak (VI.86–89). It is not merely "liberty" in whose name the rebel angels rebel but those regal values of "honour, dominion, glory and renown" (VI.420–423). Since Satan's "return," as he claims it is, is not a return but a first encounter with hell, we are meant to understand that Satan is deluded, and later he talks of the possibility of coming closer to the "ancient seat" of heaven. The terms of angelic rank are couched in the language of hierarchy ("thrones," "imperial powers"), and it is Satan's reluctance to suffer a change in these titles (so that he and his followers would become "Princes of Hell") that leads to his final act of rebellion, the plot to invade the earth and corrupt mankind. The very terms of his last deadly task are described as the fulfillment of his royal role:

> Wherefore do I assume
> These royalties, and not refuse to reign,
> Refusing to accept as great a share
> Of hazard as of honour, due alike
> To him who reigns, and so much to him due
> Of hazard more, as he above the rest
> High honoured sits?
>
> (II.450–456)

Milton's point is that high rebellion is monarchical, and little short of pretending to be a god, which is how the fallen angels then regard Satan. They do this because they both dread the mission and do not wish to undertake it themselves; they are also awed by Satan's sheer monarchical presence. At lines 468–470, Milton has Satan awing his followers into silence lest their offering to serve might make them his rivals. In this way the economy of monarchical authority is made manifest, and it is one that relies of course upon silent deceit, intimidation, and fear induced by both rulers and ruled. In *Paradise Regained,* Satan is still the "great dictator" of the fallen angels (I.113). It is no surprise, then, that Charles II's licenser of the press thought the reference to the view that solar eclipses presaged doom to monarchies (*Paradise Lost,* I.596–599) was subversive and considered erasing the passage. In the *Pro Populo Anglicano Defensio Secunda* (May 1654), Milton had indeed attacked Saumaise's claim that kings were coeval with the sun's creation (*CPW,* IV.ii.326).

Book I of *Paradise Lost* delivers an unmistakable picture of the way in which monarchs fall into disastrously wicked ways, as the fallen angels are compared to, or seen to be continuous with, the wrecked trail of monarchy. Book I recounts the history of the fallen angels as the monstrous kings of world history, often worshipped as idols. This perspective repeats to some extent in Book XII, where monarchs are child-murderers in order to protect their own succession—even King Solomon, "that uxorious king, whose heart though large,/Beguiled by fair idolatresses, fell/To idols foul" (I.444–446). Idolatry tends to destroy itself, to become unwrapped in history, often violently. When the Philistines captured the Ark of the Covenant, their idol Dagon was discovered toppled over, with hands and head cut off—an act of iconoclasm recorded in the Old Testament, but one that would not have disgraced the Reformation period (1 Sam. 5:4; *Paradise Lost,* I.457–463). Idolatry, says Milton, produces rebel kings, like Jeroboam (I.484), while the building of Pandemonium in hell is likened to what in his view is one of the grossest acts of idolatrous monumentalizing, constructing the pyramids (I.692–699). Belial is associated with untrammeled courtly lust ("a spirit more lewd/Fell not from heaven" [I.490–491]), matching the charge of adultery Milton laid at the feet of Charles I's defender Alexander More, whom he also described as a Priapus in the *Pro Populo Anglicano Defensio Secunda* (*CPW,* IV.i.575, 607).

This long passage stands in contradistinction to the lines on kingship in *Paradise Regained,* Book II, where the Son rejects Satan's temptation to worldly kingship by redefining kingship as inner control, a fusion of Christian and Stoic ideals. The "hazard" boasted by Satan is converted into a self-sacrificing, enduring humility:

> a crown,
> Golden in show, is but a wreath of thorns,
> Brings dangers, troubles, cares, and sleepless nights
> To him who wears the regal diadem,
> When on his shoulders each man's burden lies;
> For therein stands the office of a king,
> His honour, virtue, merit and chief praise,
> That for the public all this weight he bears.
> Yet he who reigns within himself, and rules
> Passions, desires, and fears, is more a king.
>
> (II.458–467)

And those who are subject to "passions, desires, and fears" without inner governance are tyrants: the fallen angels and Satan, living in their inner hells, wondering lost and perplexed. Just so Satan takes hell with him ("myself am hell" [*Paradise Lost*, IV.75]), and contains within himself the depth beyond all depth that threatens to devour him entirely. The sublimity of elevation in fact becomes its opposite: "While they adore me on the throne of hell,/With diadem and sceptre high advanced/The lower still I fall, only supreme/In misery" (IV.89–92). During the war in heaven in Book VI, the fallen angels believe that they are gods, a delusion that fulfills God's description of them in Book III.

III

Yet one of the theological centers of *Paradise Lost* is that God is undeniably king in heaven and requires obedience—undeniable to all except Satan and his followers. Only at the end of time will God cease to be a ruler, since he will then be "all in all" (III.339–341). In Book I, a fallen angel's analysis may be theologically erroneous, but he and we do not challenge the identity of the victor:

> O prince, O chief of many thronèd powers,
> That led the embattled seraphim to war
> Under thy conduct, and in dreadful deeds
> Fearless, endangered heaven's perpetual king;
> And put to proof his high supremacy,
> Whether upheld by strength, or chance, or fate.
>
> (I.128–133)

Whatever Milton's objection to kingship on earth, however close to tyranny he saw it tending, there was a heavenly king who was to be given spiritual obedience.

The license in *Paradise Lost* for Raphael to liken "spiritual things to corporal" means that Satan's rebellion is figured as a republican revolt against imposed monarchy. Nowhere is this more startlingly expressed than in King Moloch's rousing call to overwhelm God's throne:

> No, let us rather choose
> Armed with hell flames and fury all at once
> O'er heaven's high towers to force resistless way,
> Turning our tortures into horrid arms
> Against the torturer; when to meet the noise
> Of his almighty engine he shall hear
> Infernal thunder, and for lightning see
> Black fire and horror shot with equal rage
> Among his angels; and his throne itself
> Mixed with Tartarean sulphur, and strange fire,
> His own invented torments.

(II.60–70)

Let there be no mistake of the sheer daring of these lines: Milton has one of his characters imagine the destruction of God, one of the departure points in the poem for the founding of some important Romantic literary ideas.[3] But long before we have heard Raphael's explanation of the "language of accommodation" in Book V, urging us to take what we hear as a kind of allegory, we are overwhelmed by the impression of God as monarch and heaven as a monarchical, hierarchical world. After God's eschatology lecture in the first half of Book III, the angels show their approval by bowing "lowly reverent" toward the thrones of both God and the Son, cast down their own crowns in front of them (III.349–352), and then sing praises to the "Eternal king" (III.374). Even if the terms are not precisely monarchical, mankind's Fall often seems an antimonarchical revolt: "man disobeying,/ Disloyal breaks his fealty, and sins/Against the high supremacy of heaven" (III.203–205). The angelic hierarchy of neomonarchical powers will all worship the Son as universal king (for example, III.320, V.590–591), just as Mammon contemptuously refers to such "enforced" adoration (II.237–246). As if we might miss the point, Abdiel's angry demonstration of loyalty to God from within the ranks of Satan's followers rails: "Shalt thou give law to God, shalt thou dispute/With him the points of liberty, who made/Thee what thou art, and formed the powers of heaven/Such as he pleased, and circumscribed their being?" (V.822–825).

Does this mean that the Son is an earthly as well as a heavenly king, as some of the millenarians of Milton's day, who expected an imminent Second Coming of Christ, believed? The only king of the world who speaks, wearing the "likeness of a kingly crown," is Death (II.673, 696–699), although Sin proclaims Satan monarch of the earth at X.375. Satan's understanding of God's monarchy is as if God were an earthly monarch: "But he who reigns/Monarch in heaven, till then as one secure/Sat on his throne, upheld by old repute,/Consent or custom and his regal state/Put forth at full" (I.637–641). By Book X, God has degenerated in Satan's eyes to a "tyrant" (X.466). Might it not also be inferred that Satan is jealous of the creation and elevation of the Son precisely because he is inured to hierarchical habits, as well as because the Son is a "king anointed"? He might have benefited from Milton's treatises on education, grammar, and logic, all designed to break the mental bondage of custom. With Satan's rebellious followers travels the "great hierarchical standard" once the common possession of the angelic ranks (V.701). Perhaps it is altogether too unconvincing for God to say that he fears defeat unless quick defensive arrangements are made (V.729–732), but does this make him more like an earthly king in heaven than a spiritual king? Elsewhere Satan calls God the "ethereal king" (II.978), but in respect of God's taking territory from Chaos in order to create the earth. Beelzebub thinks erroneously that God wishes to conquer hell:

> for he, be sure
> In heighth or depth, still first and last will reign
> Sole king, and of his kingdom loose no part
> By our revolt, but over hell extend
> His empire, and with iron sceptre rule

> Us here, as with his golden those in heaven.
> What sit we then projecting peace and war?
>
> (II.323–329)

In God's view, the true king on earth is the Son: it will be his reward for his willingness to atone for man's sins:

> Here shalt thou sit incarnate, here shalt reign
> Both God and man, Son both of God and man,
> Anointed universal king, all power
> I give thee, reign for ever, and assume
> Thy merits; under thee as head supreme
> Thrones, princedoms, powers, dominions I reduce:
> All knees to thee shall bow, of them that bide
> In heaven, or earth, or under earth in hell.
>
> (III.315–322)

Milton is talking in a spiritual sense here, which would seem finally to put him at a distance from the millenarians of his day, who expected a literal return of Jesus as king. But still in Book V.664, the Son is "Messiah king anointed" who has introduced new laws, as if the Son's creation and crowning were like the projected Second Coming. Satan's revulsion at idolatrous behavior is continuous with Milton's own feeling toward monarchs: "every soul in heaven/Shall bend the knee, and in that honour due/Confess him rightful king" (V.816–818). Working out what this means is the problem posed to us as readers and to Satan the misreader of *Paradise Regained.* The passage discussed here ends with the fiery events of the Last Days, and Book XII in *Paradise Lost* similarly associates the reign of Jesus with the millennium that will precede the final judgment, once again a return to a vision of the Son as an earthly as well as spiritual king.

Paradise Regained picks up some other antimonarchical themes first voiced in *Comus,* including an aversion to courtly luxury and extravagant expenditure. In this world, riches do not matter:

> Among the heathen, (for throughout the world
> To me is not unknown what hath been done
> Worthy of memorial) canst thou not remember
> Quintius, Fabricius, Curius, Regulus?
> For I esteem those names of men so poor
> Who could do mighty things, and could contemn
> Riches though offered from the hand of kings.
> And what in me seems wanting, but that I
> May also in this poverty as soon
> Accomplish what they did, perhaps and more?
> Extol not riches then, the toils of fools,
> The wise mans cumbrance if not snare, more apt
> To slacken virtue, and abate her edge,
> Then prompt her to do aught may merit praise.
> What if with like aversion I reject
> Riches and realms; yet not for that a crown,

Golden in show, is but a wreath of thorns,

Brings dangers, troubles, cares, and sleepless nights.

(II.443–460)

In *Paradise Regained,* Book III, Satan identifies the Son as an earthly king who will, he suggests, rise in arms and challenge the occupying Roman forces (III.150–158). Although, as the Son points out, Satan knows that the Son's inheritance of his kingdom means his final defeat, he continues to insist that the Son view the kingdoms of the earth. What follows is a catalogue of monarchies, beginning with ancient Assyria (III.270–283) and its king Nebuchadnezzar, the nemesis of the Israelites. Through all this description the only way in which the Son can apprehend the grandness of these ancient monarchies is by a telescopic view of the massed numbers of royal armies, a visual display meant to tempt the Son into the kind of rebellious war that led his ancestor King David to victory over the Philistines. It will, says Satan, be a kingdom that stretches from Egypt to the River Euphrates. And as the Son says, while the time of his kingdom had not yet arrived (III.396–397), many of the inhabitants of the world are unworthy of a true king. In Book IV, Satan offers to give the Son all the kingdoms of the world, "On this condition, if thou wilt fall down,/ And worship me as thy superior lord" (IV.166–167)—a shallow offer that is refused. And the Son points out that Satan has been "permitted" these kingdoms by God, the ultimate king. The phrasing is a little unsettled: "Permitted rather, and by thee usurped" (IV.183), which in itself seems rather inconsistent, raising questions again about the status of God as king.

Monarchy vexed Milton and was a major imaginative stimulant in his work. Indeed, it so vexed him that its coordinates come to the reader in a series of confusingly intermixed opposites in *Paradise Lost*. Its continuing presence in his work is an admission of the hold of singular authority on the imagination and the institutions of early modern Europe, even as earthly kings are subjected within Milton's writings to iconoclastic condemnation. After the violence and bloodshed caused by European monarchs, Milton hoped for a better world, better government, better international relations:

> so many thousand Christians destroyed, should lie unaccounted for, polluting with their slaughtered carcasses all the land over, and crying for vengeance against the living that should have righted them. Who knows not that there is a mutual bond of amity and brotherhood between man and man over all the world, neither is it the English sea that can sever us from that duty and relation: a straighter bond yet there is between fellow-subjects, neighbours, and friends.
>
> *(The Tenure, CPW, III.214)*

He also hoped for better poetry. So why didn't he make God a republican?

5

FREE STATES

> The cleerest and absolutest
> free nation in the world
> —*The Readie & Easie Way, CPW,* VII.446

I

In the midcareer comments made in the *Pro Populo Anglicano Defensio Secunda* (May 1654), Milton said that while many minds had set to work on the civil and religious dimensions of the national crisis in the 1640s, he had chosen to confine himself to domestic issues and the matter of freedom of the press (*CPW,* IV.i.621–627). He was speaking from a position of some assurance: although he had been completely blind for more than two years, and although he had lost his first wife and a son, he was the senior civil servant in the Office for Foreign Tongues and he had been rewarded with a house in Petty France (a street in Westminster near the center of government). There was clearly discernible in his thought a political theory that grew in significance and that can be glimpsed in the tracts from the 1640s onward, and in the poetry too. The burden of reading so much historical literature and law in the later 1640s created a risk of detracting from the impetus provided by Milton's earlier grounding in ancient political theory and its ideas of liberty and citizenship. Furthermore, Milton's view of freedom had uncomplicated origins. The idea that freedom or liberty was the opposite state from slavery, and that in this state of liberty free men were required to exercise their freedom in self-constituting acts of public and private virtue, was known to Milton at an early stage in his career. Its most famous exponent in Renaissance Europe was Cicero.

Thus, while the debates surrounding the civil war were concerned with the origins of sovereignty (for the Parliamentarians they were in the people) and the grounds for resisting a tyrant, questions that, as we have seen, take up much space in *The Tenure of Kings and Magistrates,* another set of issues was moving toward the foreground of Milton's attention. The apparent slowness for full-grown republican theory to emerge is typical of this period. There were comparatively few committed republicans, with developed views on the issue, before a republic arrived, de facto, in January 1649, with the execution of the king and the abolition of the House of Lords (although many more knew about republican ideas). The Rump Parliament was effectively (much to the discontent of many of its members) a republican regime, with a single chamber as its representative and the Council of State as its executive body. Milton is among the first in the history of political thought, if not the very first, to argue that a republic is to be preferred at all costs to a monarchy, as opposed to seeing both as different elements of one single (post-Aristotelian) constitution.[1]

The positive account of the history of political society in *The Tenure* (as opposed to the account of tyranny) looks like a fusion of radical Puritan views of biblical freedom and Aristotle's political theory. Mankind was born free and lived so in Eden, but the Fall resulted in wrongdoing and violence. It was necessary to combine in civil society in order to have security, and subsequently necessary for the business of upholding laws for single figures, called magistrates but sometimes kings, who were not overlords but "Deputies and Commissioners, to execute, by virtue of their entrusted power, that justice which else every man by the bond of nature and of covenant must have executed for himself, and for one another" (*The Tenure, CPW,* III.199). From here, further corruption resulted in magistrates becoming tyrants, with the consequence that both oaths and parliaments were then invented as a bridle on the potentially unlimited power of kings.

The 1650s were a time of intense debate on the nature of the best republican constitution for England: how many representative bodies and at what levels of the social order; the extent to which the constitution had to be an appropriate reflection of the social relations in the nation at large, not least the property relations. Whatever Milton thought about institutions, he left them alone in any great detail in his published writing until the very late 1650s, when England was on the verge of the return to monarchy—well alone, apart from several defensive statements designed to point up the elective nature of the republic's institutions, such as the small council that was deemed necessary for administration (*Pro Populo Anglicano Defensio, CPW,* IV.i.317). As an apologist for the regicide and as an administrator, he was keen on administrative efficiency. But mostly he made several statements in praise of the heroic spirit that was required in a free state. In this way, he has usually been seen as the ideologist of virtue for the English republic and Protectorate, pointing up the practice of liberty by his contemporaries in a value economy where an excess of heroic virtue exemplifies the free state and pleases God. The sentiment is evident in the sonnets and sonnet-related poems of the mid-1640s, decrying Presbyterian censoriousness, and forged most startlingly in the panegyric on Fairfax and Cromwell, the soldiers who won the civil wars, and Sir Henry Vane, the Puritan-republican hero of toleration. They have been seen as a fusion of Petrarchan form and the idealism resident therein with Horace's praise of political rectitude:

> O yet a nobler task awaits thy hand;
>> For what can war, but endless wars still breed,
>> Till truth, and right from violence be freed,

And public faith cleard from the shameful brand
Of public fraud.

("On the Lord General Fairfax at the Siege of Colchester,"
lines 9–13 [8 July–17 August 1648], *CSP*, 323–324)

The sonnet on Vane is more politically perceptive in its delineation of the different aspects of the public sphere, marrying an allusion to Machiavelli (iron, not God, is the sinew of war) with the separation of religion and politics:

to advise how war may best, upheld,
Move by her two main nerves, Iron and Gold
In all her equipage; besides to know
Both spiritual power and civil, what each means,
What severs each, thou hast learnt, which few have done
The bounds of either sword to thee we owe;
Therefore on thy firm hand Religion leans
In peace, and reckons thee her eldest son.

("To Sir Henry Vane the Younger,"
lines 7–14 [June–July 1652], *CSP*, 330–331)

The sonnet to Vane was intended for manuscript circulation within the corridors of the republic's administration. Nonetheless, it begins to contain the simplicity of diction that marked other sonnets, such as "On the late Massacre in Piedmont" (? June 1655), which may have been intended for publication in a printed news book and hence designed to be read by a broader readership. Sonnets to Edward Lawrence and Cyriack Skinner (both written in 1655) celebrate the same liberty as well as friendship in rich poetry, and poetry is offered as an act performing liberty in the Commonwealth, just as in the *Pro Populo Anglicano Defensio Secunda* it is the people who have made an epic of themselves by heroically casting off their oppressor, inviting the poet to follow epic decorum and begin *in medias res:*

> As the epic poet, if he is scrupulous and disinclined to break the rules, undertakes to extol, not the whole life of the hero whom he proposes to celebrate in his verse, but usually one event of his life (the exploits of Achilles at Troy, let us say, or the return of Ulysses, or the arrival of Aeneas in Italy) and passes over the rest, so let it suffice me too, as my duty or my excuse, to have celebrated at least one heroic achievement of my countrymen. Who could extol the achievements of an entire nation?

> (*CPW,* IV.i.685)

The poet in turn embodies as a prophet a vision of national destiny:

> Now, surrounded by such great throngs, from the Pillars of Hercules all the way to the farthest boundaries of Father Liber, I seem to be leading home again everywhere in the world, after a vast space of time, Liberty herself, so long expelled and exiled. And, like Triptolemus of old, I seem to introduce to the nations of the earth a product from my own country, but one far more excellent than that

of Ceres. In short, it is the renewed cultivation of freedom and civic
life that I disseminate throughout cities, kingdoms, and nations.

(*Pro Populo Anglicano Defensio Secunda, CPW,* IV.i.555)

The defenses were written in Latin and designed for a European
audience. They drew widespread revulsion and rebuttal in a great
number of writings from western and central Europe, from the Med-
iterranean to the Baltic, and copies were publicly burned, for instance, in Paris and Toulouse. They were nonetheless admired for
their eloquence, even by monarchs like Queen Kristina of Sweden,
and by the mid-1650s, Milton knew that he was a famous name on
the continent. It was imperative that the defenders of monarchy
prove him wrong, since he had drawn English nationhood and republicanism together in a rhetorically powerful conjunction. Thus, as
late as 1674, amplifying a text written first in 1651, the Hamburg ju-
rist Johann Slüter argued in an appendix to his *De subjecto summae
potestatis in imperio seu republica Rom. Germanica* that Milton's description of the English Commonwealth was in fact wrong: the true
description was to be found in the Elizabethan Sir Thomas Smith's
Re Republica Anglorum (1583), a work that defends English mixed
monarchy. Milton certainly bought into the presentation of the English state as the ancient ideal of a balanced combination of monarchy,
aristocracy, and democracy when it suited him, until the late 1650s,
so it is significant that Slüter saw a departure in earlier writings.

Milton also worked in the early 1650s as a licenser and oversaw some of the material that went into the government news book, *Mercurius Politicus*. Royalists gleefully pointed out that the former spokesman for free speech was now a book censor. In this context he was also involved with attempts to generate a genuinely republican literary culture. His admirer John Hall played a central role in the attempt to attract dispossessed and imprisoned royalists, who were given the opportunity to exchange their literary services for freedom or material gain. It was a state-sponsored patronage system, and although Milton's uncompromising stances meant he would not have been sympathetic to many of the authors approached by Hall, who were often happy to defend the republic but were often anti-Puritan, the situation helps to explain the apparent echoes in his poetry from these years of work by other writers, like Marvell. We can also see a meeting of the literary idealism of the republic's men of letters, which was not necessarily ideological, with their political loyalties. The chief interests of the republican writers included, for example, Lucan, the Latin poet of the civil war between Julius Caesar and the republic, and, in the case of John Hall, a more obscure but nonetheless remarkable attempt to translate Sappho's poetry into English. Hall's important translation of Longinus's *On the Sublime,* in which elevated poetry is seen to flourish best in a free state, was the inspiration for several famous poems from the era, such as Marvell's *An Horatian Ode.* Milton's joining of Petrarch and Horace in his sonnets on Fairfax and Vane, and in the sonnet on Cromwell, is part of this movement. His 1650s writings are patent exercises in the elaboration of a republican sublime, even down to *Paradise Lost,* which was quickly recognized as the most conspicuously sublime poem of the era. Part of this sublimity was produced by remodeling Lucanic verse, a kind of paradoxical epic poetry because "real history." Because the republic was short-lived, and because the literary giants of the succeeding generations, like Dryden, were so determined to erase its memory, we have lost all sense of its presence in history. But it *was* there.

How much Milton understood about the workings of a free state, as opposed to its ideal spirit, and what he would have learned from his role as secretary for foreign tongues are another matter. *The Readie & Easie Way to Establish a Free Commonwealth* appeared in two editions in February and early April 1660. The "good old cause" was very nearly lost by then, as the restoration of the monarchy was only a few weeks away. Milton was at pains to halt this slide toward monarchical thinking within Parliament—not a forlorn idea, since it seems that in the nation at large there was no great enthusiasm for a return to monarchy. Quite simply, the various experiments in nonmonarchical government had not produced a durable alternative, and Milton's dismay with the succession of Parliaments since 1649, as well as with many aspects of Protectorate government, put him at one with many of his countrymen.

His solution was an envisioned republic of virtue, in which stability was achieved by the avoidance of elections, a proposal that sounds decidedly less liberal than the image of vigorously productive citizens in *Areopagitica.* Milton's worry was that there would be a return to "old bondage," nourished by "cunning deceivers," and his solution was one election that would return a godly, republican representative. There would then be no further elections, but with a virtuous representative in place, dying members would gradually be replaced with others who had learned their virtuous godliness and their oratorical power through participating in church meetings and local assemblies. These would therefore be acting as the training ground for the guardians of the nation. Milton's answer for why a stable Parliament and government had not arrived blames disaffected persons and ambitious army leaders (as opposed to the body of soldiers) and the fears that successive Parliaments would destabilize the Commonwealth. In the second edition of *The Readie & Easie Way,* he accordingly rejects both the principle of rotation in assemblies and the idea of two assemblies, proposed by the major republican theorist James Harrington (*CPW*, VII.435). An unchanging representative bespeaks an immortal commonwealth, he claims, and he looks to other free states to justify his view: ancient Israel, Greece, Rome, Venice, and the United Provinces. Wherever there is an assembly with regular elections, so also there will be, he argues, a permanent assembly of some kind. It is a devolved vision, with every chief city being the head of a particular region, itself a "little commonwealth."

Another important aspect of *The Readie & Easie Way* was that there should be absolutely no interference of the state in religious matters. In addition to adhering in this way to what Milton regarded as biblical precept, it would also, he argued, create a quiet state.

II

Milton's republican precepts are laid out in the clearest parts of his poetry. The vision of history given by Michael to Adam in Book XII of *Paradise Lost* includes the episode of Nimrod (XII.24–62), presented as the first tyrant, who "not content/With fair equality, fraternal state"—the benign patrician republics of the postdeluvian world—"Will arrogate dominion undeserved/Over his brethren, and quite dispossess/ Concord and law of nature from the earth." Adam learns that after the Fall, with the loss of "rational liberty" and the fusion of "right reason" and "true liberty," tyranny is always possible, and God has decided to subject fallen man, who has lost his inward liberty, to the external privations of "violent lords." The passage connects with the biblical symbolism of the time, Nimrod attaching to several powerful figures in seventeenth-century England: Charles I, Cromwell, Charles II. Nimrod is responsible in Milton's version for the Tower of Babel, which Milton took to be an emblem of the unfinished commonwealth in *The Readie & Easie Way* (*CPW*, VII.357). The history of the Israelites plays up the assembly (the Sanhedrin), even as God gives the laws directly to Moses. The Israelite kings who start with David end with Jesus Christ, the king who reigns forever, enabling Milton to fuse republican and sacred historiography. The villains of the Israelite world are the priests, the Presbyterians of their day, and the superstitious Roman Catholic clergy that preceded them.

To this could be added the visions of strife given to Adam in Book XI, all the result of a failure of wisdom, virtue, and gifts for the sake of "effeminate slackness" (XI.634). Adam has been learning about death and its consequences. These later sections of *Paradise Lost* fit with, and in some instances may have been written after, *Paradise Regained*, which is more coherently republican in character. Here the Son is subjected to Satan's temptations of wealth and power in the middle books of the poem. Part of the hunger experienced by the Son might be for riches, Satan suggests toward the end of Book II. The Son replies that wealth is nothing without virtue, valor, and wisdom and then offers a typically republican account of how the greatest men have come from nothing and expected less despite their triumphs. The Son names four such famous Roman heroes—Lucius Quintius Cincinnatus, Gaius Fabricius Luscinus, Manius Curius Dentatus, and Marcus Atilius Regulus—although it is also significant that they were celebrated by Saint Augustine too (II.446). The second temptation is one of empire, at the start of Book III, in which Milton's elitism is certainly mixed, since the Son rejects empire, glory, and fame but spurns the people, "a herd confused,/A miscellaneous rabble" (III.49–50). The classical republican objection to empire is also evident in these lines:

They err who count it glorious to subdue
By conquest far and wide, to overrun
Large countries, and in field great battles win,
Great cities by assault: what do these worthies,
But rob and spoil, burn, slaughter, and enslave
Peaceable nations, neighbouring or remote,
Made captive, yet deserving freedom more
Then those their conquerors, who leave behind
Nothing but ruin wheresoe'er they rove,
And all the flourishing works of peace destroy,
Then swell with pride, and must be titled gods,
Great benefactors of mankind, deliverers,
Worshipped with temple, priest, and sacrifice.

(III.71–83)

The villains here are Alexander the Great and Scipio Africanus. Later on Satan tries another tactic, suggesting to the Son that he liberate his people and hence become their king. The Son's reply may be read as a reminder that he is ultimately under divine injunction, as are we: nothing can be done without obedience to God. But "All things are best fulfilled in their due time" (*Paradise Regained,* III.182) also suggests the Italianate republican ideal of *occasione,* waiting for the optimum time to bring in a proper order in the state.

Satan's final attempt in Book III to woo the Son with an image of the monarchies of the world is remarkable for its cinematic quality. We do not see buildings but a series of major conflicts taking place, the reader being permitted to view both large panoramas and small details at once. At the end even a reference to a siege in Boiardo's *Orlando Innamorato* (1495) is worked in (III.337–343), but the general tenor of the passage is more in keeping with Lucan's pro-republican epic of the war between the republicans under Pompey and Julius Caesar, *De bello civili.* Satan offers the Son, if he is to be the king of Israel, the strategy of conquering the Parthians in order to be secure against the Romans. These are later versions of parallels that Milton had once seen between England and Rome: the Parliament had negotiated with the king, as Rome had sent a delegation to Mark Anthony. God had nonetheless delivered the English from their slavery, whereas the moment in ancient history marked the end of Roman freedom (*Pro Populo Anglicano Defensio, CPW,* IV.ii.332).

In Book IV, Satan improves in seeming republican strategy, presenting Rome through the microscope that is also a telescope (IV.57), but it is a Rome that despite its architectural splendor is corrupt in the person of its aged and retired emperor, Tiberius. Satan offers the Son the chance to redeem Rome. And the Son's castigation of Rome itself is absolute:

> That people victor once, now vile and base,
> Deservedly made vassal, who once just,
> Frugal, and mild, and temperate, conquered well,
> But govern ill the nations under yoke,
> Peeling their provinces, exhausted all

By lust and rapine; first ambitious grown

Of triumph that insulting vanity;

Then cruel by their sports to blood enured

Of fighting beasts, and men to beasts exposed,

Luxurious by their wealth, and greedier still,

And from the daily scene effeminate.

What wise and valiant man would seek to free

These thus degenerate, by themselves enslaved,

Or could of inward slaves make outward free?

(IV.132–145)

What is clear in *Paradise Regained,* which was probably intended as a guide to interpreting *Paradise Lost,* is quite the opposite in the longer, earlier poem. As we have seen, if Satan is presented as a tyrant, he is also a republican hero. The fallen angels debate their predicament not only in terms of a lost kingdom but also in terms of lost republican liberty. They suffer "equal ruin," but this is better than bowing before the throne of God. And of course, "Here we may reign secure, and in my choice/To reign is worth ambition though in hell:/ Better to reign in hell, then serve in heav'n" (*Paradise Lost,* I.261–263). Satan has achieved his status, he says, through "merit" rather than inheritance. Hell appears to be governed by "popular votes," which incline to the fallen angels remaining there. Satan argues against the "popular vote," in line with Milton's contempt for vulgar opinion (II.313). The parliament in hell is a perpetual assembly, just as Milton advocates a perpetual parliament in *The Readie & Easie Way.*

But the recalled Long Parliament of 1659 had brought back those members excluded in 1649 who had opposed the trial of the king. In 1660 they "crept lately out of their holes, their hell . . . by the language of their infernal pamphlets, the spew of every drunkard, every ribald" (*The Readie & Easie Way,* 2d ed., *CPW,* VII.452). In April 1660, in Milton's view, Parliament was in hell. Milton's description of the psychological forces at work inside the English Parliament chimes with the debates in the infernal parliament in Book II. This negative portrayal of the powers of debate is related to Milton's sense that the English were very bad indeed at grasping the advantages that Providence held out to them. Thus, although Milton's *History of Britain* (1670), two thirds of which was written in the late 1640s, stops before the Norman conquest, the message in history for Milton is clear. This was enforced by the "Digression" concerning the Long Parliament attached to the *History.* It used to be thought that this castigation of Parliament's resolve was written with regard to the events of spring 1660. But now a persuasive case has been made for 1649 as the date of composition: Milton laments the Long Parliament's inability to found a true free state after the removal of the tyrant. The cause was lost as soon as it was won.

Moloch's speech in *Paradise Lost,* Book II, offers classical republican liberty as an antidote to the "splendid vassalage" of being in heaven, "preferring/Hard liberty before the easy yoke/Of servile pomp" (II.255–257). The lines have been seen as an echo of Aemilius Lepidus's objection to the dictator Sulla in Milton's favorite Roman historian, Sallust, who documented the decline of Rome from liberty to servitude in his *Bellum Catilinae.* Satan evokes the sanctity of choice in suffrage, as, after the debate, the fallen angels decide what to do. But as we have seen, Satan's "monarchal pride" overawes any resistance to his plan of revenge. It has not, after all, been a free debate. The fallen angels believe Satan is their savior; in the end, they will suffer a greater loss in their subterranean exile. Nonetheless, these terms of liberty are the way in which Satan persuades the fallen angels to rebel with him. The "new laws" that have come in with the creation of the Son are an imposition of monarchy on those who hitherto lived as equals, despite the fact that the angels are organized in orders and degrees. Satan's claim to have no knowledge of the creation ("We know no time when we were not as now" [V.859]) may be symptomatic of his fall, but it is also a denial of the moment of origin so crucial to most patriarchal and monarchist thinking. By offering a "steady state," a "self-begot, self-raised" version of angelic history (V.860, I.634), Satan also avoids a focus on moments of state formation—moments that deeply attracted the republicans and the new theorists of absolute sovereignty, especially Hobbes. They are, of course, highly creative moments.

These terms continue in the war in heaven, recounted in Book VI. The possibility that the war in heaven might refer to the pamphlet wars of the 1640s, especially the puns connecting ordinance with discourse (VI.558–627), is reinforced by Milton's picture of himself in the *Pro Populo Anglicano Defensio Secunda* as a soldier armed for combat with a pen against the republic's enemies: "When he with insults was attacking us and our battle array, and our leaders looked first of all to me, I met him in single combat and plunged in his reviling throat this pen, the weapon of his own choice" (*CPW*, V.i.556). The rebel angels master artillery; hateful as it is, it was associated with the New Model Army (VI.482–489). Here Satan speaks the language of republican liberty as it had come down to the Italian Renaissance, and in particular the works of Machiavelli and his commentary on Livy's history of Rome, the *Discorsi*. Machiavelli had been adopted by the English republicans for his description of the vigor that was required of Englishmen in order to regain their liberty. Milton had read Machiavelli; there is evidence of much reading in the Commonplace Book, and Machiavelli would, courtesy of Milton's sometime acquaintance and fellow republican Marchamont Nedham, become influentially present in *Mercurius Politicus*. Machiavelli and godliness do not to the modern mind go easily together, and it is not hard to see why, after secular republicanism had apparently failed, one might wish to portray Machiavellianism in a negative way. So Satan to Abdiel: "now/I see that most through sloth had rather serve,/Ministering spirits, trained up in feast and song;/Such hast thou armed, the minstrelsy of heaven,/Servility with freedom to contend" (VI.165–169).

The fallen angels believe that empire has followed from the rise of monarchy in heaven. Indeed, Raphael talks of God's "eternal empire" (VII.96), even when republicans saw empire as a form of tyranny. The Protectorate's adventures against the Spanish in the Caribbean in the mid-1650s, known as the Western Design, were unpopular with many republicans. Before the Fall, one of Satan's identities is as a conquistador. He looks upon the sun as the possessor of the world with "sole dominion," but the intent of his voyage of discovery from hell is to steal it. His approach to Eden is likened to that of a Portuguese trader, who first is lost in the Indian Ocean, then, placing the voyage at an earlier stage, rounds the Cape of Good Hope, passes Mozambique, and approaches the spice lands of the East. His imagined approach to Adam and Eve is the lie of colonial exploitation, to make an alliance for the sole purpose of benefiting the colonialist: "League with you I seek,/And mutual amity so strait, so close,/That I with you must dwell" (IV.375–377). After the Fall, Adam and Eve are represented as native Americans, waiting to be Columbus's prey, and there are other negative references to Spanish colonial activities in the Americas (IX.1115–1118). And yet, conversely, the creation is represented as a territorial wresting of matter away from Chaos, the poem effectively describing the progressive encroachment on Chaos's original demesne by hell and earth in addition to heaven.

It should now go without saying that Milton sought a Christian commonwealth. If God is king in heaven and the Son the universal king on earth in a spiritual sense, how can political freedom and religious liberty be seen to coexist? Furthermore, how can political theory and theology meet? In a sense, they should not. Milton published two treatises in 1659 dedicated to the absolute separation of church and state: *A Treatise of Civil Power in Ecclesiastical Causes* (February 1659) and *Considerations Touching the Likeliest Means to Remove Hirelings* (August 1659). No interference from the state should take place in ecclesiastical matters, where discussion should be drawn entirely from biblical precept. Milton aligns himself with the Puritan reform movement of the 1650s, aiming to abolish the tithing system so that at last church funding would be voluntary and all connection with a worldly establishment would be severed:

> Let whoso will interpret or determine, so it be according to true church discipline; which is exercised on them only who have willingly joined themselves in that covenant of union, and proceeds only to a separation from the rest, proceeds never to any corporal enforcement or forfeiture of money, which in all spiritual things are the two arms of Antichrist, not of the true church; the one being an inquisition, the other no better than a temporal indulgence of sin for money, whether by the church exacted or by the magistrate; both the one and the other a temporal satisfaction for what Christ hath satisfied eternally; a popish commuting of penalty, corporal for spiritual; a satisfaction to man, especially to the magistrate, for what and to whom we owe none.
>
> (*A Treatise of Civil Power, CPW,* VII.249)

Tithes remained in place, however, and in 1662 the reinstituted Church of England was bolstered by the Act of Conformity, which compelled nonconformist divines either to renounce their principles to keep their livings or to be ejected. Milton's later poetry supports the nonconformists, or Dissenters, as they became known, and is full of messages of succor for them. On the war plains of heaven, Abdiel claims to speak for a sect (*Paradise Lost*, VI.147). This necessarily brought into question the relationship between religion and the state, even as church-state separation was so desired: Milton rebuts Alexander More's charge that equality in the state is an Anabaptist doctrine and says instead that it is drawn from ancient democracy (*Pro Populo Anglicano Defensio Secunda, CPW,* IV.i.633). So what is a spiritual democracy, and can it exist?

What brings men together in *Paradise Regained* is that they all have the chance to become sons of God, by imitating the Son himself. From this path Satan is excluded, as he is unable to interpret who is the Son of God. He thinks it is himself:

> In what degree or meaning thou art called
> The Son of God, which bears no single sense;
> The Son of God I also am, or was,
> And if I was, I am; relation stands;
> All men are Sons of God; yet thee I thought
> In some respect far higher so declared.

(IV.516–521)

But the Son proves him wrong. "All men are Sons of God," rephrasing Matthew 6:9, is the sentence that defines Christian liberty and the potential for a truly free state in the poem. And without religious freedom there can be no sonship: "It plainly appear, that if we be not free we are not sons, but still servants unadopted; and if we turn again to those weak and beggarly rudiments, we are not free; yea, though willingly and with a misguided conscience we desire to be in bondage to them; how much more then if unwillingly and against our conscience?" (A Treatise of Civil Power, CPW, VII.266). Shortly after this passage Milton reads the episode of Ishmael, son of the bondwoman Hagar, and how they are cast out in the desert and saved by an angel (Gen. 21:9) as an allegory of persecution, following Saint Paul's reading of it in this way in Galatians 4:29. The same example is worked into Paradise Regained, II.305–315, now offered implicitly as advice to the persecuted Puritans.

Milton's final published prose work, Of True Religion (1673), may have been pitched more conservatively to encourage consensus among Protestants, with large areas of possible disagreement, all framed by a common commitment to the authority of the Bible, with willingness to return to it again and again for guidance in debates. This is a common English Protestant theme, but that frame of reference is very, very broad, including by name Lutherans and Calvinists but stretching out to Anabaptists, Arians, Socinians, and Arminians, all of whom were in one way or another anathema to official faith in

1673. By association, *Paradise Regained* is a far more significant document in the history of toleration than might at first appear to be the case.

Milton needed radical Puritanism, and in particular his version of the idea of sonship, to make his vision of history and his theory of action in the world complete. Thus the apparent pacifism in *Paradise Regained* qualifies the injunctions to violent resistance in *Samson Agonistes*, which are nonetheless never quite dismissed. We might need them after all to defend liberty. In any case, the Son never entirely loses sight of worldly politics, and with Samson spirituality is never far from the reader's purview. Liberty partakes of energy, and its realization is heroic: a noble force against slavery, tyranny, and empire. But in addressing debate and hearing and satisfying all views, heroic efficiency may be fatally compromised. In political affairs, when the moment comes, as Machiavelli said, seize it, but "trying all things" may raise passions fit only for hell.

6

IMAGINING CREATION

I

Space: the final frontier. Adam asks Raphael to narrate the creation of the universe at the start of *Paradise Lost*, Book VII:

> relate
> What may no less perhaps avail us known,
> How first began this heaven which we behold
> Distant so high, with moving fires adorned
> Innumerable, and this which yields or fills
> All space, the ambient air.
>
> (VII.84–89)

And the creation of nearly everything in the universe comes from God himself, *ex deo*, because God is nearly everything that is in space:

> Boundless the deep, because I am who fill
> Infinitude, nor vacuous the space.
> Though I uncircumscribed my self retire,
> And put not forth my goodness, which is free
> To act or not, necessity and chance
> Approach not me, and what I will is fate.

> (VII.168–173)

In orthodox theology, God created out of nothing, *ex nihilo*, which also means that whatever the "nothing" was, it had nothing to do with him. But to create out of himself means logically that everything that exists was originally part of God—the matter of God, so to speak. The creation of the earth and everything therein, including the humans, is designed to repopulate heaven. God says that the race of men will eventually return to heaven by merit (the Fall and its consequences are interestingly absent in this passage) and make up the deficit left by the fallen angels, surrounding God with his own substance, sufficiently refined (VII.150–160).

But what actually happens when the world is created? We've already seen the striking way in which creation is described as "divorce" and how that relates to Milton's divorce arguments . Milton is playing some games of near-deception, and we have to be watchful. The agent of creation is actually the Son, who is equivalent at this point with the Word: "my Word, begotten Son, by thee/This I perform, speak thou, and be it done" (VII.163–164). So in fact the Son does the creating, and he is given physical shape for us as a kind of heroic charioteer, with the Holy Spirit standing beside him: "My overshadowing spirit and might with thee/I send along, ride forth, and bid the deep/Within appointed bounds be heaven and earth" (VII.165–167). These lines have been used as evidence that Milton was an orthodox Trinitarian, and so it seems, for the Son and Spirit are performing the acts of creation, united with God and apparently in the Godhead. But Milton calls it the "filial Godhead," which means that there is within it an inferiority relationship, at the very least: there is a father and a son. And when the Son passes through the gates of heaven to do the creating, he does not look much like the Son as we have seen him: "to let forth/The king of glory in his powerful Word/And Spirit coming to create new worlds" (VII.207–209). So is the Son the "king of glory," or is he God himself?

When the business of creation is done, the Son returns to heaven. It is as if he has indeed become God: "The great creator from his work returned/Magnificent, his six days' work, a world" (VII.567–568). To do this is to commit one of the greatest acts of heresy, giving human form to that which is beyond such animation, an idolatrous act beyond all imaginable blasphemy. This is a direct consequence of Milton's development of his mythic account of creation. The narrative suggests Trinitarian dimensions, but especially since we know that these ideas are also challenged, godliness in the sense of the power of creation falls on a figure who is not God and who has been given human dimensions during the course of creation. The tension of identities within the poem is evident in a sentence that has notoriously confused editors:

> The filial power arrived, and sat him down
> With his great Father (for he also went
> Invisible, yet stayed, such privilege
> Hath omnipresence) and the work ordained,
> Author and end of all things.

(VII.587–591)

Early editors made "Father" the subject of "ordained" and hence the "author and end," but Hebrews 12:2 refers to Christ as "author and finisher," in the sense of man's redeemer. Some have felt that the biblical echo elevates the Son's role in the creation, with the Son as the subject of the sentence.

The Son is portrayed as mythic maker, ripe for William Blake's famous painting:

>   in his hand
> He took the golden compasses, prepared
> In God's eternal store, to circumscribe
> This universe, and all created things:
> One foot he centred, and the other turned
> Round through the vast profundity obscure,
> And said, Thus far extend, thus far thy bounds,
> This be thy just circumference, O World.

(VII.224–231)

This is in fact a repetition of God's creation of heaven (VII.232), a little detail that Milton slips in, and in doing so he drastically qualifies the rather simpler statement in Genesis 1:1. If we start reading just a few lines later, we miss the crucial role of the Son, since at line 243 Milton picks up on the first actual command of God in Genesis 1:3: "Let there be light, said God, and forthwith light/Ethereal, first of things, quintessence pure/Sprung from the deep." But it is still the Son who has been there doing the scene-shifting. God is naming in heaven, but the Son is acting on the earth, a distinction that disappears from view at this point.

The fact that it is God and not the Son who does the naming allows Milton to follow a far more conventional description of the creation of the elements, nature, and the animals. The Bible is a strong source here, as are popular vernacular creation poems, especially Joshua Sylvester's translation of the French Protestant du Bartas's *Les Semaines* (1578–1603; trans. 1592–1608). Perhaps the Son's role is more evident at the point where man is created (VII.519–534), but Raphael's narration doesn't at this stage go into details. Nonetheless, God speaks "audibly" to the Son, addressing the joint project: "Let us make now man in our image" (VII.519). And man is created, we are told three times in this short passage, in the image of God, as a "similitude." Does this mean that God is a guy, visible in a human form, lessening the sense we have in Book III that angry God is a metaphorical portrayal of the incomprehensible? The charge against some of the English Socinians, the anti-Trinitarians whom Milton broadly supported, was that they had anthropomorphically depicted God, as opposed to accepting scriptural metaphor as a necessary way of explaining sacred matters to sublunary and frail intelligences.

The problem continues with the role of the Son, and in particular his intercession. Milton has to reinvent the atonement, especially since he downplays the crucifixion. In Books III and X–XI, the atonement occurs as a conversation between God and the Son, in which the Son offers to undergo death in order to pay the ransom for mankind's sins. And in Book X, it is not God, or, accurately speaking, "the voice of the Lord God" (Gen. 3:8), who confronts Adam and Eve after their temptation but the Son. Adam and Eve hear the voice of God, but it is the Son who makes contact possible by being physically present (X.85–102). As the Son facilitates the voice of God in Eden, promising that the seed of the woman will bruise the serpent's head (Gen. 3:15), so he is able to see the future when Jesus will defeat Satan, a passage (X.182–192) that resembles the closing movement of *Paradise Regained.*

A more extensive episode of intercession occurs early in Book XI, when the Son is moved by the penitent prayers of Adam and Eve. Milton bases his text, it has been argued, on Hebrews 9:24, where Christ is imagined "to appear in the presence of God for us." This refers to Christ's ascension after his resurrection, and some of the Socinians imagined this to mean that Christ interceded on behalf of mankind after his crucifixion. Since they also believed that the Son was created when he was born of a woman, the episode as Milton describes it, coming shortly after the Fall but a long time before most of the events recounted in the Old Testament, cannot in their view have taken place. It has been conjectured that the Son's intercession in this way is in fact an adaptation by Milton of the Socinian position, and that it is a crucial part of Milton's downgrading of the crucifixion in his explanation of the atonement.[1] After all, the Son hears the prayers of Adam and Eve, which are "engrafted" onto his own payment and then offered up to God, who receives them and grants immortal life to those who follow his ways. Adam and Eve, we are told, have been moved to prayer by the "prevenient grace" that has wafted down from heaven and that presumably has been in existence since the Son first offered himself as a redemptive sacrifice for mankind in Book III. The passion of Christ is squashed into four lines and seemingly replaced in significance with an immediately postlapsarian intercession. We can see in Milton's text the kinds of objections made to the Socinian position. With grace bought at this point, why did the Son need to die? And in making Adam and Eve so active in unwinding the consequences of the Fall, isn't Milton denying the special place of Christian witness and, even more, showing little difference between Jews and Christians?

In *Paradise Lost* so much poetic energy has been directed at showing the proximity of unfallen man to God and of giving human shape to the Son, if not also to God, that we begin to feel an anthropomorphizing energy throughout the poem, as its total argument comes together in our minds. Thus, at the sentencing of man in Book XI, man's crime is to have become like God and the angels: "like one of us man is become" (XI.84). To eat the fruit of the Tree of Life would be to live forever, or, so Milton adds to Genesis, to "dream at least to live/For ever" (XI.95–96), which seems to repeat how things were before the Fall anyway. But the point here is the proximity in standing of the "sons" of God (XI.84)—the angels and mankind, and, with a more distant prospect, the fallen angels, yet more "sons," once blessed. How far are we from the story of the sons of God in the pseudepigraphical Book of Enoch (known to Milton through a Latin translation by the Dutch humanist Vorstius), who came down from a mountain, made love to the women, and bred a race of giants, or to the early commentaries on Genesis 6 that assumed fallen angels had mated with women (Milton alludes to the scripture at XI.621–622)? Adam and Eve first appear as "Godlike erect," meaning, we initially suppose, that they are as beautiful as the pagan gods (IV.289–290). But can that be right? Aren't they made in the image of God, and hasn't Milton slipped to saying that they look like him? When Adam says that in his dream he could see that Eve was less a resemblance of God than he was (VIII.543–544), isn't he talking in the most literal of senses?

Waking as a son of God is how one might describe the conversation between Adam and Raphael, especially by the time it reaches its climax in Book VIII. Adam "new waked" (VIII.4) suggests the new creation enjoyed by post-atonement man, and although Raphael urges Adam to confine his inquiries into the nature of the universe to earthly matters, the very fact that his Copernican and Galilean questions have been made points up an apparent closeness between man and angels, humans and divine beings in an atmosphere of "wonder . . . delight, and . . . glory." Adam's questioning is rendered in poetry of intelligent astronomical speculation:

> When I behold this goodly frame, this world
> Of heaven and earth consisting, and compute,
> Their magnitudes, this earth a spot, a grain,
> An atom, with the firmament compared
> And all her numbered stars, that seem to roll
> Spaces incomprehensible (for such
> Their distance argues and their swift return
> Diurnal) merely to officiate light
> Round this opacous earth, this punctual spot,
> One day and night; in all their vast survey
> Useless besides, reasoning I oft admire,
> How nature wise and frugal could commit
> Such disproportions, with superfluous hand
> So many nobler bodies to create,
> Greater so manifold to this one use,
> For aught appears, and on their orbs impose.
>
> (VIII.15–30)

It is then matched by Raphael's no less curious excursion through different models of astronomical explanation. "Contented that thus far hath been revealed" (VIII.177) is how Adam is reported to have been left, but the reader has been entirely woken up by this speculation; we feel that our minds are living as never before. The mind wanders and must be checked, but it will wander, because it is made in the image of God and yearns to ride with him: "apt the mind or fancy is to rove/Unchecked, and of her roving is no end,/Till warned, or by experience taught, she learn" (VIII.188–190).

It is just as well that Adam has such mental powers. Since Raphael wasn't present at the creation of man, he is glad to hear Adam narrate it. Adam's recounting of his creation is as much a gesture of wonder and love to posterity as it is to Raphael. Who does Adam see in his dream—the guide of "shape divine" who takes him to the nuptial bower? Is this "shape divine" another angel, the Son, or even God? It is probably the latter, giving the wording of lines 316–317. Indeed it is an apparently wonderful being who creates Eve by opening Adam's left side; it is all a kind of lovemaking in the sense of the love of the creator for his creation. Although asleep, Adam witnesses the creation of Eve through an inward mental awareness, like that of a partial anesthetic, yet he is conscious enough to see "the shape/Still glorious before whom awake I stood." And all to culminate in the consummation of the paradisal marriage, and an uneasiness where sexual passion is acknowledged ("transported I behold,/Transported touch; here passion first I felt,/Commotion strange" (VIII.529–531). Raphael warns that this is deceptive and bestial and might spoil the proper exercise of free will; far better to find "true love," which "refines/The thoughts, and heart enlarges" (VII.589–590). Is this not what we have just witnessed between God, angel, and man, requiring a supreme act of loving from God, who, after all, is solitary? Now we see the trick: passion has just been redefined. No longer is passion the act of suffering in the crucifixion; now it is the desire of the first man for the first woman. No small event in the history of semantics (Milton is particularly on the ball here; the *Oxford English Dictionary* gives the first dating for "passion" meaning sexual desire as 1641), and, as it were, the end of the act of God's creation, rather than the response to Satan's sometime victory.

II

There is another creation that happens in Milton's epic before the creation of the earth, and that is the creation of Pandemonium in hell. This is the beginning of a series of creations that will last through Book II, before we meet God in Book III. Pandemonium arises as a response to the call for renewed war against heaven (I.661–662), begun by Moloch (whom we learn was known in the ancient world as Mulciber and Vulcan [I.740]). It is made from impure gold and imagined as a kind of music, with many ribs of the structure rising from molds in the grounds of hell like so many notes played simultaneously on an organ, and with the secondary sense of the organ pipes as a visual comparison to the ribs. This was probably a rather sobering parody of the praise by Milton's poet friend Andrew Marvell of Lord Protector Oliver Cromwell as a magnificent political architect, playing the state into being, as Amphion raised Thebes with his lute.[2]

Pandemonium is built so that the fallen angels can debate their course of action, and the result is that Satan begins his arduous journey to earth in order to bring the new race of humans to ruin. The journey then is part of anticreation, relative and in opposition to God's creation. The first obstacles Satan meets are the locked gates of hell, guarded by the monstrous figures of Sin and Death. As we will learn, they are Satan's creation. Where Pandemonium is tainted gold, Sin and Death are, within the terms of Milton's allegorical verse, distorted forms: a woman once fair, now turned into a serpent, but with an open vagina into which the "hell hounds" bred from her incestuous rape by Death perpetually and periodically return, and a black shapeless shape wearing a crown: "shape it might be called that shape had none/Distinguishable in member, joint, or limb,/Or substance might be called that shadow seemed,/For each seemed either" (II.667–670). Death has an even greater capacity to change shape than Satan, and they threaten to engage in tumultuous combat when they are interrupted by Sin, who solves the issue by reminding Satan of that which he has forgotten: his original rebellion was the thought that gave her birth. It is a passage in which Milton describes painful mental stirring on Satan's part as a precedent of the creation of Eve by God from Adam's side. Coming from Satan's head, Sin is a beautiful woman and a thought:

> Hast thou forgot me then, and do I seem
> Now in thine eye so foul, once deemed so fair
> In heaven, when at the assembly, and in sight
> Of all the seraphim with thee combined
> In bold conspiracy against heaven's king,
> All on a sudden miserable pain
> Surprised thee, dim thine eyes, and dizzy swum
> In darkness, while thy head flames thick and fast
> Threw forth, till on the left side opening wide,
> Likest to thee in shape and countenance bright,
> Then shining heavenly fair, a goddess armed
> Out of thy head I sprung; amazement seized
> All the host of heaven; back they recoiled afraid
> At first, and called me Sin, and for a sign
> Portentous held me; but familiar grown,
> I pleased, and with attractive graces won
> The most averse, thee chiefly, who full oft
> Thyself in me thy perfect image viewing
> Becam'st enamoured.

(II.747–765)

And they had an affair "in secret" with "joys/Then sweet," apparently, as the war in heaven began, which resulted in the birth of Death.

What is behind the allegory? Rebellion is the creation of a woman and the consequent birth of "anti-matter" (Death), which brings all substance to ruin. (Similarly, in *Samson Agonistes*, Dalila has a "child" from her coition with Samson: treason.) Certainly the allegory generates appropriate connotations for the theology of the poem: remorse and guilt, for instance. The poetry seems to exist entirely in its own realm, behind which there is nothing discernible as an allegorical referent. It is what it is, and its reference to massive things in physical and conceptual size makes the episode conspicuous as an example of sublime poetry. The creation with words has reached this irreducible extent. This is no more evident within the world of the poem than in the creation by Sin and Death of the bridge from hell to earth, presumably made from hellish material, a conduit for evil spirits to enter and leave the earth, and physically a manifestation of the dead waste of the universe, just as Death, we learn, is happy at the endless consumption his presence on earth will permit. Moreover, the allegory fuses at its margin with non-allegory, converting the latter in the reader's eyes into the indubitably sublime poetry of this section:

> Then both from out hell gates into the waste
> Wide anarchy of chaos damp and dark

Flew diverse, and with power (their power was great)
Hovering upon the waters; what they met
Solid or slimy, as in raging sea
Tossed up and down, together crowded drove
From each side shoaling towards the mouth of hell.
As when two polar winds blowing adverse
Upon the Cronian sea, together drive
Mountains of ice, that stop the imagined way
Beyond Petsora eastward, to the rich
Cathaian coast. The aggregated soil
Death with his mace petrific, cold and dry,
As with a trident smote, and fixed as firm
As Delos floating once; the rest his look
Bound with Gorgonian rigour not to move,
And with asphaltic slime; broad as the gate,
Deep to the roots of hell the gathered beach
They fastened, and the mole immense wrought on
Over the foaming deep high arched, a bridge
Of length prodigious joining to the wall
Immovable of this now fenceless world
Forfeit to death; from hence a passage broad,
Smooth, easy inoffensive down to hell.

(X.282–305)

To create is also to seize material from Chaos, and in this respect the
epic yokes the imperial themes of exploration with the cosmological

reapportioning necessary for creation that Chaos himself resists. Not for the first time do we find ourselves in sympathy with Satan as he battles through the contesting elements of Chaos in search of the earth. After all, it nearly defeats him: "on all sides round/ Environed wins his way; harder beset/And more endangered (II.1015–1017). It is for Milton a poetic triumph in which he imitates not merely Ovid's representation of chaos but also the energetic, atomistic poetry of Lucretius. Both are surpassed by the mythopoeia of Satan's final triumphant journey (only the second to last time he will have a triumph) through the adversity of the elements:

> He ceased; and Satan stayed not to reply,
> But glad that now his sea should find a shore,
> With fresh alacrity and force renewed
> Springs upward like a pyramid of fire
> Into the wild expanse, and through the shock
> Of fighting elements, on all sides round
> Environed wins his way; harder beset
> And more endangered, than when Argo passed
> Through Bosporus betwixt the jostling rocks:
> Or when Ulysses on the larboard shunned
> Charybdis, and by the other whirlpool steered.
> So he with difficulty and labour hard
> Moved on, with difficulty and labour he;

> But he once past, soon after when man fell,
> Strange alteration!

(II.1010–1024)

At the end of his journey through Chaos, Satan "lands" on the outer sphere ("the firm opacous globe" [III.418]) that surrounds the earth (and contains the stars and the planets) in the universe as Milton conceives of it. What had seemed a globe in distance is now experienced by Satan as a waste wilderness. While we are impressed with the epic similes of Satan as vulture waiting to prey on the young of sheep and goats and as a Chinese land ship, we also confront the fact that Milton is describing space travel. As Satan "walks" on this "surface" (for it is a surface appropriate for his substance), Milton uses his experience of God's creation as the lens through which we gain this knowledge. Satan is therefore a figure for education at this point in the poem. It is through Satan that we view Milton's Protestant limbo, created by the "vain things" that fly up from the earth into the higher atmosphere, which is empty but waiting for recipients in the future history of mankind. Even with nothing present for Satan to confront, we are shown a colorful collection of monstrosities, the begetters of outrageously proud projects like Babel and mistaken philosophers, to say nothing of the hosts of Roman Catholic religious orders, or, more alarmingly, those whose faith is so misguided they make an earthly pilgrimage rather than seek immediate access to God. All will be denied access to heaven:

And now Saint Peter at heaven's wicket seems
To wait them with his keys, and now at foot
Of heaven's ascent they lift their feet, when lo
A violent cross wind from either coast
Blows them transverse ten thousand leagues awry
Into the devious air; then might ye see
Cowls, hoods and habits with their wearers tossed
And fluttered into rags, then relics, beads,
Indulgences, dispenses, pardons, bulls
The sport of winds: all these upwhirled aloft
Fly o'er the backside of the world far off
Into a limbo large and broad, since called
The Paradise of Fools, to few unknown
Long after, now unpeopled, and untrod.

(III.484–497)

They have been created, but creation has rejected them.

The path from heaven to earth is Satan's opportunity, both a literal stairway and a metaphorical passage through the stars (which Satan sees "nigh hand" as other distinct worlds, "happy isles" with inhabitants). He loses sense of all dimensions, just as he did when he traveled through Chaos, and heads at first to the sun, where, says the narrator, he would be visible as a sunspot. The allusions here are to heroes of the new science such as John Wilkins, Tycho Brahe, and Johannes Kepler, as well as Ptolemy and Copernicus (but later, in Book VIII.71–84, astronomy is rebuked by Raphael), although it is on the sun that the solutions not to the astronomer's questions but to alchemy and the hermetic tradition are rendered in the shape of the philosopher's stone. Satan takes all this in with keen percipience ("Undazzled, far and wide his eye commands" [III.614]), even as in a shadowless world the rays of the sun shoot directly up from its surface. Here Satan meets Uriel, who, though sharp-sighted, is unable to detect the hypocrisy symbolized by the angelic disguise and directs the archfiend to earth. Uriel says that Satan as unfallen cherub is displaying creditable "excess" in wishing to see earth as an aspect of angelic pleasure, worthiness, and delight. "Excess" is the key, for of course Satan is all excess, which is why he has escaped from hell—an awkward fact not quite in the rulebook of the heavenly. We the readers, along the way, have had a remarkable education in cosmology, one that is aware of debates among the new scientists and that surprisingly posits the ultimate source of evil as the means by which the reader is educated, a path not without hesitation and indeterminacy.

The narrator is following Satan closely when we first see Eden. So it is in a vein of satanic voyeurism continuing from the end of Book III that we first judge paradise in Book IV, as new scientists and new world explorers. Milton does indeed represent Eden as a tropical rainforest. Pine, cedar, and fir trees surround the wall of paradise, but there are also palms, and inside,

> in this pleasant soil
> His far more pleasant garden God ordained;

Out of the fertile ground he caused to grow
All trees of noblest kind for sight, smell, taste;
And all amid them stood the Tree of Life,
High eminent, blooming ambrosial fruit
Of vegetable gold . . .
A happy rural seat of various view;
Groves whose rich trees wept odorous gums and balm,
Others whose fruit burnished with golden rind
Hung amiable, Hesperian fables true,
If true, here only, and of delicious taste.

(IV.214–219, 247–251)

Adam and Eve live in the paradisal state that many of Milton's radical religious contemporaries thought they could resurrect in this life. But before we come to paradisal marriage, we experience the very structure and grain of substance in the garden. We see into the texture of the fruit eaten by Adam and Eve, and hence further into creation: "The savoury pulp they chew, and in the rind/Still as they thirsted scoop the brimming stream" (IV.335–336). The world is beautifully present in each distinct object: "how spring/Our tended plants, how blows the citron grove,/What drops the myrrh, and what the balmy reed,/How nature paints her colours, how the bee/Sits on the bloom extracting liquid sweet" (V.21–25). The flowers are objects of heightened perception, but they are also lenses through which our vision is clarified.[3] Perhaps research in hydrodynamics was fused with Edenic optimism, as the river in its course under the hill produces a fountain which in turn helpfully waters the garden: horticultural technology and perfect nature are combined. In Book VIII, we learn that Eve has a "nursery" of plants (VIII.46). All of this is in addition to the qualities familiar to students of *Paradise Lost:* that the poet uses fallen terms to describe prelapsarian matters—"wanton locks" and "mazy error," for instance, or that the animals have innocent passions. The significance is that we appreciate the innocent use of what is for us a noninnocent word, and this points in two ways: on the one hand, to the inevitable truth that we live in time after the Fall, and on the other, to the possibility that we can come a long way to overcoming the vitiation of the Fall in this life. This is the poem's way of helping us do this, a perspective that is enhanced by the continuous angelic presence in Eden: "Millions of spiritual creatures walk the earth/Unseen" (IV.677–678).

The first section of Book VIII contains Raphael's overview of astronomical theory, with Adam willingly following his hint to leave these speculations for higher beings. That may be good enough for Adam, but is it enough for us the readers? The questions—whether the earth rises on the sun or vice versa; how the planets move; whether Copernicus's three motions of the earth are true; whether there is an invisible primum mobile—are certainly there for our contemplation. Soon we are going to see innocent, dutiful Adam failed by his faithfulness. Isn't Milton implicitly introducing double-think into his poem, suggesting that knowledge of the heavens might well help to save us in future? Milton was proposed in 1667 as a possible author for a poem on the Royal Society and its achievements.[4] Contrary to the limit Raphael imposes on Adam, the first parent is clearly an exponent of the *priscia theologia,* the idea that God had placed in Adam the uncorrupted name and knowledge of every object in creation; by looking at each one, Adam could name them. We seek through hermetic knowledge to return to this state.

Adam also argues for the partner who will help him enjoy paradise. It is easy to concur with him that this is a matter of the exercise of free will, less easy to believe that God is merely testing Adam's powers of judgment in denying him one for as long as he does. How beastly of him! And yet all this while, as we've already noticed, Adam has been talking directly with God. Raphael instructs Adam to resist the deposing of reason that Eve's attractive presence exerts over him, but it is this unbounded pull that stays with the reader: "passion . . ./Commotion strange, in all enjoyments else/Superior and unmoved, . . . All higher knowledge in her presence falls/Degraded" (VIII.530–532, 551–552). Are these not the consequence of free will (Adam's need for a partner) and desire? Does free will only have to be a regulatory power? Raphael's denial of "carnal pleasure" does not reveal an adequate understanding of Adam's feelings, which might already as "passions" be partaking of the higher love that the angel praises. After all, the angels love by having angelic intercourse (VIII.620–629).

Far from convincing us to look only within our sphere, Raphael's strictures on knowledge seem as much to spur us on to seeing further into creation, and the narrator dares to make us see Satan's part in the great rebellion that was anticreation. Whatever Milton did or did not know of science, whatever he thought of its discoveries, whatever he thought of the relationship between the authority of ancient literature and the findings of empirical observation, he propels his readers to approach the knowledge of the gods even as he strides over one and a half millennia of restrictive thinking.

7

THE LOVER, THE POEM, AND THE CRITICS

I

You would think to find in a Renaissance poet who wrote secular as well as sacred poems some expression of the torments of love, tossing and turning in the sheets upon waking in frustration at denial. You would think to find it in a sonnet, especially for a poet who admired Sidney and Shakespeare. What is more remarkable in Milton's early sonnets is the decorum exercised in imitating Petrarch. The effect is not so much a sacrifice of sincerity at the altar of form as the magnificent overtaking of mere desire by the execution of the poem, which becomes the love object itself:

> Giovane piano, e semplicetto amante
>   Poichè fuggir me stesso in dubbio sono,

Madonna a voi del mio cuor l'umil dono
Farò divoto; io certo a prove tante
L'ebbi fedele, intrepido, costante,
De' pensieri leggiadro, accorto, e buono;
Quando rugge il gran mondo, e scocca il tuono,
S'arma di sé, e d'intero diamante,
Tanto del forse, e d'invidia sicuro,
Di timori, e speranze al popol use
Quanto d'ingegno, e d'alto valor vago,
E di cetra sonora, e delle muse:
Sol troverete in tal parte men duro
Ove amor mise l'insanabil ago.

Since I am a young, unassuming and artless lover, and do not know how to escape from myself, I will make you, lady, in my devotion, the humble gift of my heart. I have proved it in many a trial, faithful, brave, and constant, graceful, wise, and good in its thoughts. When the whole world roars and the lightning flashes my heart arms itself, in itself in perfect adamant, as safe from chance and envy and from vulgar hopes and fears as it is eager for distinction of mind and real worth, for the sounding lyre and for the Muses. You will find it less hard only in that spot where love stuck its incurable sting.

(Sonnet VI, *CSP*, 98–99; translation by John Carey)

Much later this becomes the exquisite expression of a compromised person (in his blindness) mourning a dead wife, a wife whom he never saw but only touched and heard. It is a pure and Puritan poem, obstetrically acute and faithfully Petrarchan:

> Methought I saw my late espousèd saint
>> Brought to me like Alcestis from the grave,
>> Whom Jove's great son to her glad husband gave,
>> Rescued from death by force though pale and faint.
> Mine as whom washed from spot of childbed taint,
>> Purification in the old Law did save,
>> And such, as yet once more I trust to have
>> Full sight of her in heaven without restraint,
> Came vested all in white, pure as her mind:
>> Her face was veiled, yet to my fancied sight,
>> Love, sweetness, goodness, in her person shined
> So clear, as in no face with more delight.
>> But O as to embrace me she inclined,
>> I waked, she fled, and day brought back my night.
>>> (Sonnet XIX, *CSP,* 348)

The search has always been for a higher love, rejecting the physically gross in *Comus* or refining it in *Paradise Lost,* or searching for the loving relations that make sense of man's relationship with his maker.

Hence the realism of affection in *Paradise Lost:* "Sole partner and sole part of all these joys,/Dearer thyself than all" (IV.411–412). The narrator shares these sentiments of Adam:

> So spake our general mother, and with eyes
> Of conjugal attraction unreproved,
> And meek surrender, half embracing leaned
> On our first father, half her swelling breast
> Naked met his under the flowing gold
> Of her loose tresses hid: he in delight
> Both of her beauty and submissive charms
> Smiled with superior love.
>
> (IV.493–499)

Hence also the intense terror and pity of the Fall when it arrives, and the heightened emotional states of the humans that follow. Eve persuades herself that she has won a trial of love (does she realize it is between Adam's love for God, on the one hand, and for her, on the other?). The Fall of Adam proceeds as a hot and heavy lovers' session, while the earth groans. Leaving aside the fact that it was God who put the fruit of the Tree of Knowledge of Good and Evil in the garden, and God who made it so that it would induce in humans a fuggy intoxication, they wake up into a new world bereft of innocence, where shame, once a principle of internal good governance, now becomes the mark of original sin. A universe of conjugal stress will follow: "high passions, anger, hate,/Mistrust, suspicion, discord, and shook sore/Their inward state of mind"; "of their vain contést appeared no end" (IX.1123–1125, 1189).

That uncomfortable universe we see again in *Samson Agonistes,* in these lines of painful domestic disharmony:

Less therefore to be pleased, obeyed, or feared,
These false pretexts and varnished colours failing,
Bare in thy guilt how foul must thou appear!

    Dal. In argument with men a woman ever
Goes by the worse, whatever be her cause.

    Sam. For want of words no doubt, or lack of breath,
Witness when I was worried with thy peals.

    Dal. I was a fool, too rash, and quite mistaken
In what I thought would have succeeded best.

(lines 900–908)

Now Milton chooses to make Dalila bear symbolic connotations that connect with the arguments for resistance to tyrants; she has been persuaded, she says, to betray Samson by Philistine worthies who have pleaded the cause of the public good. She has alienated both the private claims of her marriage and, because Samson is a Nazarite, divine sanction. Nonetheless, the portrayal of conjugal affliction is brutally intense, and culminates in a divorce that would otherwise be uxoricide:

    Dal. Let me approach at least, and touch thy hand.
    Sam. Not for thy life, lest fierce remembrance wake
My sudden rage to tear thee joint by joint.
At distance I forgive thee, go with that;
Bewail thy falsehood.

(lines 951–955)

Samson forces all his antagonists off the stage by presence and threat, but the most sensitive relationship he has is with his father, Manoa, who understands that his son is a chosen one and who cannot brook Samson's seemingly ill-advised partnership choices—to him a matter of serial judgment failure (by contrast, Samson thinks that marrying the woman of Timna and Dalila were good ways of making war on the Philistines [lines 421–422]). Samson knows he has broken his vow with God not to reveal the secret of his strength ("Sole author I, sole cause" [line 376]). Whatever the differences between them, both have faith that God will prove Dagon a mere idol. Manoa indeed takes his son's words as a prophecy; both understand (or by the end of the play will understand) the meaning of a cause.

And this is what Milton understood as a crucial component of his republican political theory. If you are dedicated to virtue, loving your country or your people becomes the first duty or desire of both citizen and elected officer, however complicated Milton's understanding of "country" and "state" was. Thus, Milton noted Machiavelli's insistence in his *Discorsi* that those who teach religion are more important in a state than even founders of states themselves (Commonplace Book, *CPW*, I.475–476). This reference in the Commonplace Book, encompassing as it does a substantial passage from Dante's *Purgatorio* criticizing the temporal power of the papacy, explains the attraction of the Italian political thinker to seventeenth-century English republicans, and surprisingly places a category of love into a set of observations usually thought to be secular or even "atheist." Perhaps we might even say in Miltonic terms that Machiavelli refinds "love" and that Milton knows this, even if the terms of Machiavelli's belief in popular participatory politics go beyond the degree of popular participation permitted in Milton's mature republican vision (Commonplace Book, *CPW*, I.477).[1]

Loving your state and loving your creation are what is exhibited most positively throughout *Paradise Lost*. God shows sheer delight when he understands that the Son is prepared to sacrifice on behalf of mankind: "O thou/My sole complacence! well thou knowst how dear/To me are all my works" (III.275–277). "Because in thee/Love hath abounded more then glory abounds" (III.311–312), the Son will be made universal king of everything, on earth as well as in heaven and in hell, and God links this proclamation of love directly with the Son's final triumph in the Last Judgment, the incineration of the world, and the creation of "New heaven and earth," this time not ruled by the Son, since government will now cease. The fire seems like a purging of all that has been accumulated as "unjust" in the creation, a culmination of all of the "downwards"-moving substances throughout the poem, neutral or evil. Will Satan, the fallen angels, and hell finally be annihilated in this process? Does a free-will universe, if it persists in the new creation, mean there will be another angelic rebellion?

The love of divinity for human works elicits a reciprocal response.

The conversation between Raphael and Adam in Book VIII is especially charged, Eve's absence (and subordination) notwithstanding, by the fact that Adam is effectively speaking to the voice of origin, even if mediated through a narrating archangel. It is nothing less than a high expression of human love for humanity's creator: "For while I sit with thee, I seem in heaven,/And sweeter thy discourse is to my ear" (VIII.210–211). Creating is an act of love to be met by a reciprocal devotion; it is a theological point, and one suited to a poet who so stressed the *felix culpa,* or fortunate fall. Now with the Son as "filial Godhead" doing the actual creating at God's command, we don't see very much of what happens:

> he formed thee, Adam, thee O man
> Dust of the ground, and in thy nostrils breathed
> The breath of life; in his own image he
> Created thee, in the image of God
> Express, and thou becam'st a living soul.
>
> (VII.524–528)

We don't see much more when Adam recalls the creation of Eve, a kind of surgery-cum-butchery that turns from gastronomy to artistry:

> I saw,
> Though sleeping, where I lay, and saw the shape
> Still glorious before whom awake I stood;
> Who stooping opened my left side, and took

> From thence a rib, with cordial spirits warm,
> And life-blood streaming fresh; wide was the wound,
> But suddenly with flesh filled up and healed:
> The rib he formed and fashioned with his hands;
> Under his forming hands a creature grew,
> Manlike, but different sex, so lovely fair.
>
> (VIII.462–471)

More interesting, then, is the preceding conversation between God and Adam, in which God teases Adam by delaying Eve's creation in order to make the first human reflect upon solitude, which is God's state, in a mini-trial. Though under a holy anesthetic of sorts, Adam still sees in his imagination not only Eve's creation but also "the shape/Still glorious" with whom he has companionship.

Milton's ideal godly republic, outlined in *The Readie & Easie Way* (March 1660), has the sense of untroubled perpetuity that attaches to the briefly mentioned new creation—too lacking in turbulence by half. The history of the world and of heaven is continually marked by energies all of which are generated by some kind of love, or the kind of angry love that is associated with passion. No greater lover of God was there than Satan; or did he love himself too much? The revolt in heaven grew out of a sense of displacement on Satan's part by the creation of the Son. In hindsight, it looks like an act of love that brings forth love and that tests obedience, a test that Satan fails. Satan's rebellion in the name of an unjust relegation and a spurning is also a matter of forgetting one's creation, forgetting one's origin and therefore the being to whom one owes everything:

> who saw
> When this creation was? Rememberst thou
> Thy making, while the maker gave thee being?
> We know no time when we were not as now;
> Know none before us, self-begot, self-raised
> By our own quickening power, when fatal course
> Had circled his full orb, the birth mature
> Of this our native heaven, ethereal sons.
>
> (V.856–863)

Regarding existence as a function of thought, Satan represents himself as a Cartesian, and more traditionally exhibits the sin of wishing to exist autonomously. His original name has been lost (it was probably not Lucifer), and "envy," "pride," and "impious rage" seem wholly inconsistent with the zeal and love that are generally born in heaven (V.593). Certainly Milton's poem gives us instant "deep malice" in Satan, but that seems caused by spurned love, an instant transformation on account of rebellion. Satan is obeyed by the soon-to-be fallen angels because they are obedient; rebellion comes out of fealty, and Abdiel's attempt to stay the war in heaven has failed. Then follows in time after Satan's defeat and expulsion from heaven the things we've already learned from earlier in the poem: the anger at defeat, the despair and the creeping sense that defeat is an irreversible fate, that partial victory is only greater defeat, that all attempts to come close to God's love again will lead only to a more painful sense of exclusion. Satan "could love" Adam and Eve, so close are they to divine resemblance, and so evidently showing the shape of their creator. Instead, however, it is jealousy he feels, and the desire for revenge, tempered nonetheless by sympathy and wonder at their innocence, all mixed together in a frightful and untrustworthy mess that can mean only death and more death:

> To you whom I could pity thus forlorn
> Though I unpitied: league with you I seek,
> And mutual amity so strait, so close,
> That I with you must dwell, or you with me
> Henceforth; my dwelling haply may not please
> Like this fair Paradise, your sense, yet such
> Accept your maker's work; he gave it me,
> Which I as freely give; hell shall unfold,
> To entertain you two, her widest gates.

(IV.374–382)

You cannot erase the antilove of Satan, or his strange kind of love, certainly not if as a poet you love your creation as God loves his creatures. Finally, then, and in the most intellectualized sense of the word, Milton loves his language—the English language, and drama

---

at that. What we witness through this great career and so many works, and through such a polyglot capacity, is a poet's love for the civility and civilization embodied in the language he has made his own, the creature of his creation. Through the perpetuation of these works and their extended appreciation over time, the forces of tyranny and empire, of censorship, manipulation, and exploitation, are to be challenged, overcome even, with the teachings of free will.

II

In this way, the achievement of the poetry and of *Paradise Lost* in particular is to offer to the reader a new Bible, one that recasts key biblical figures, stories, and aspects of theology. The novelist Philip Pullman has been deeply influenced by Milton's theology. But in his annotated edition of *Paradise Lost,* it is poetic excellence that he singles out: "No one, not even Shakespeare, surpasses Milton in his command of the sound, the music, the weight and taste and texture of English words."[2] Satan moves into prominent place, however difficult and self-divided his character, as Milton gives us good and evil coming into the world together. That Milton dares to use forbidden knowledge, not only, as we have seen, as a theme, but also in terms of the textual architecture of the poem, underwrites this. Were it not for the centrality of Adam and Eve, we might be forgiven for seeing the poem as a more balanced struggle between Satan and the Son. The narrative weight of the poem pulls in the direction of Satan; we are pulled the other way, abruptly sometimes, even unconvincingly, by the narrator and God's statements. The Son acts against Satan as an epic deus ex machina, the most decorous, and to the modern reader the most artificial, of poetic modes. It is Christian epic, but it is also, from an orthodox viewpoint, heretical and full of forbidden knowledge, through and through.

Pullman's comment reminds us that *Paradise Lost* is also a *literary* Bible. Its capacious construction suggested to early readers that it was a map of literary history and a guide to literary values in a way that no work in English had quite been. The allusion to mythic figures, the personae from pagan theology, and the imitation or adaptation of ancient or merely earlier verse forms are bound up with the free-will theology of the poem and the issues of cultural memory and degeneration that come with it. The grim history of mankind delivered by Michael at the end of the poem is a contextualizing device for the exciting reinventions of epic description that we find earlier.

The rest of the poem works like this too. Milton's richest poetic achievement is probably his description of the Garden of Eden in Book IV. We see it though the eyes of Satan: "Beneath him with new wonder now he views/To all delight of human sense exposed/In narrow room nature's whole wealth" (IV.205–207). The description of the *locus amoenus* is an exemplary European Renaissance garden, a "woody theatre" (IV.141), and outdoes all previous literary examples even as it alludes to them:

A heaven on earth: for blissful Paradise
Of God the garden was, by him in the east
Of Eden planted; Eden stretched her line
From Auran Eastward to the royal towers
Of great Seleucia, built by Grecian kings,
Or where the sons of Eden long before
Dwelt in Telassar: in this pleasant soil
His far more pleasant garden God ordained;
Out of the fertile ground he caused to grow
All trees of noblest kind for sight, smell, taste;
And all amid them stood the Tree of Life,
High eminent, blooming ambrosial fruit
Of vegetable gold.

(IV.208–220)

Soon the unfallen irrigation system, whereby water rises rather than falls from the sky, is described, the air is permanently, pleasantly perfumed, and the reader comes to understand that he is viewing the garden as if it were a landscape painting. And indeed Milton responds to the new trends in painting of his day, particularly innovations by Dutch painters. First the garden affords a "prospect" (IV.144). Then, in the first edition, of 1667, line 153 reads Dutch *lantskip*, because the English word "landscape" had not yet properly emerged; it was in fact a technical term in Dutch art. By line 340, Milton has become confident enough to issue a twelve-line reference to the painterly topos of the animals in Eden. The perfumed air is offset with a reference in lines 166–171 to the story of Tobias and the Angel, from the apocryphal Book of Tobit. Here Tobias wished to marry Sara, a Median woman. She had been married seven times already, but before consummation could happen a jealous spirit called Asmodeus had killed each of her husbands. The archangel Raphael advises Tobias to burn the entrails of a fish to ward off the spirit. The episode foreshadows Satan's eventual defeat, since Asmodeus was bound and taken off to Egypt. While it might seem odd to compare Edenic odors with "fishy fume" (line 168), the fact is that Adam and Eve will not have such a pungent remedy against Satan, and that will be too bad.

It is a comforting thought that the three Graces dance with the "Hours" (seasons) at lines 267–268 in perpetual motion to signify the movement underlying all natural generation, or that Venus is present, through reference to her attributes of myrtle and mirror (IV.262–263). With them is "universal Pan," associated in Renaissance symbol systems with Christ, but in the following famous sentence Eve in Eden is implicitly compared to a series of ancient stories concerning rape, metamorphosis to avoid rape, and sexual jealousy. It is in fact a far from happy prospect. Eden might be wonderful, but the textual Eden is interwoven with a record of abduction and defloration:

> Not that fair field
> Of Enna, where Prosérpin gathering flowers

Her self a fairer flower by gloomy Dis
Was gathered, which cost Ceres all that pain
To seek her through the world; nor that sweet grove
Of Daphne by Orontes, and the inspired
Castalian spring, might with this Paradise
Of Eden strive; nor that Nyseian isle
Girt with the River Triton, where old Cham,
Whom Gentiles Ammon call and Lybian Jove,
Hid Amalthea and her florid son
Young Bacchus from his stepdame Rhea's eye;
Nor where Abassin kings their issue guard,
Mount Amara, though this by some supposed
True Paradise under the Ethiop line
By Nilus' head, enclosed with shining rock,
A whole day's journey high, but wide remote
From this Assyrian garden, where the fiend
Saw undelighted all delight, all kind
Of living creatures new to sight and strange.

(IV.268–287)

In respect to the first smile, Milton probably had in the forefront of his mind Ovid's account of the rape of Proserpine (*Metamorphoses,* V.385ff.). Ovid himself forgot to mention that Proserpine was abducted at the point at which she plucked a narcissus plant, although this is mentioned in the earlier Greek Homeric Hymn to Demeter. Because Milton is squashing four parallels into one poetic sentence, he apparently has no space to mention the pomegranate that Proserpine ate in Hades, which kept her there for an extra period (she was forbidden to eat while in the underworld) and which appears in both the Hymn to Demeter and Ovid. The plucking of the narcissus and the eating of the pomegranate prefigure, of course, the temptation of Eve, so to the informed reader the incomplete allusion stands out like a sore thumb. It puts pressure on the coherence of Milton's free-will theology (since for a brief moment we lose sight of it), and also on Milton's knowledge of poetic tradition, which itself is also part of a free-will universe. Ovid has a memory failure in neglecting the narcissus, and Milton sustains that loss or absence. Furthermore, the story's explanation of the formation of the seasons (Proserpine is finally commanded by Zeus to spend one third of the year with Dis) is also absent. Rape is textually present as Eden is described, and in any case, there is a degree of suppression in the full details of the mythic parallel. The syntax hurries us along with its catalogue of "nor's," but only to be stopped at the figure and gaze of Satan "where the fiend/Saw undelighted all delight" (IV.285–286). When we come to the lake scene, in which Eve is delighted with her reflection but then led away by a voice to meet Adam (IV.460–471), it is the voice of the New Testament (Col. 2:17) which comes to correct Ovid, Eve being inserted into a version of the Narcissus episode (*Metamorphoses*, III.402–436).

By the time we come to the nuptial bower itself, Milton apparently overcomes the negative freight of the Pandora story, which he explicitly mentions, with the sheer power of evoked innocence in the description of Edenic delight:

> underfoot the violet,
> Crocus, and hyacinth with rich inlay
> Broidered the ground, more coloured then with stone
> Of costliest emblem: other creature here
> Beast, bird, insect, or worm durst enter none;
> Such was their awe of man. In shadier bower
> More sacred and sequestered, though but feigned,
> Pan or Silvanus never slept, nor nymph,
> Nor Faunus haunted. Here in close recess
> With flowers, garlands, and sweet-smelling herbs
> Espousèd Eve decked first her nuptial bed,
> And heavenly choirs the hymenean sung,
> What day the genial angel to our sire
> Brought her in naked beauty more adorned,
> More lovely than Pandora, whom the gods
> Endowed with all their gifts, and oh too like
> In sad event, when to the unwiser son
> Of Japhet brought by Hermes, she ensnared
> Mankind with her fair looks, to be avenged
> On him who had stole Jove's authentic fire.

(IV.700–719)

This is wonderful verse, bringing together appeals to all the senses and nicely pivoting on the identity of the genial, or generative, angel, whose identity is not disclosed (at lines 467–475 it is a voice, and later, at VIII.484–487, Adam claims that Eve was led to him by God). It looks forward to the roses showered on the sleeping, postcoital Adam and Eve of lines 772–773. The roses in the bower's roof are perpetually replaced, and their descent suggests sexual spending, as well as being a further painterly reference to Botticelli's *The Birth of Venus*. The roses are picked up at the start of Book V with "Morn her rosy steps" (line 1), and this echoes the iconography of another Botticelli painting when, like Zephyrus, the wind god, to Flora in *Primavera*, Adam whispers gently to Eve (lines 15–16).

Book V takes us beyond painting into the beginning of an explanation of the nature of creation. At its beginning, the emotional tenderness between Adam and Eve is unmatched in any part of Western literature. Yet the references to Pandora, Epimetheus, and Prometheus, found earliest in Hesiod's *Theogony*, 570 ff., where Pandora's opened box let every evil into the world, allowing Jupiter to be revenged on mankind for Prometheus's theft of heavenly fire, leave a very nasty taste in the mouth. Indeed, in a similar but lighter comparison in *The Doctrine and Discipline of Divorce* (August 1643), Eve is absent: Pandora represents free will (*CPW*, II.293). Logically, in fact, it raises the possibility of gods who will vengefully punish mankind.

These overtones are evident earlier in the book. At the very start
of Book IV, we meet Satan discovering that he cannot escape hell,
since it will travel with him and in a sense is him. We will see Eden
through Satan's eyes, but it is an astonishing revelation beforehand of
his remorse. The intensity of his inner turmoil (likened to a cannon
recoiling within him as it fires) is set against the calm despair of that
remorse, and he defies the sun by claiming to be able to remember
the future (IV.25):

> O thou that with surpassing glory crowned,
> Lookst from thy sole dominion like the God
> Of this new world; at whose sight all the stars
> Hide their diminished heads; to thee I call,
> But with no friendly voice, and add thy name
> O sun, to tell thee how I hate thy beams
> That bring to my remembrance from what state
> I fell, how glorious once above thy sphere;
> Till pride and worse ambition threw me down
> Warring in heaven against heaven's matchless king:
> Ah wherefore! He deserved no such return
> From me, whom he created what I was
> In that bright eminence, and with his good
> Upbraided none; nor was his service hard.

(IV.32–45)

Rebellion is disdainful, but it is also now entirely within the realm of
the understandable: "lifted up so high/I sdeigned subjection, and

thought one step higher/Would set me highest, and in a moment quit/The debt immense of endless gratitude" (IV.49–52). More evident is Satan's rapid pace toward paradise and his quick thwarting of Eden's wall. Nor will it be indifferent verse that sees Satan make his approach to Eve, but more of the magnificent same:

> So spake the enemy of mankind, enclosed
> In serpent, inmate bad, and toward Eve
> Addressed his way, not with indented wave,
> Prone on the ground, as since, but on his rear,
> Circular base of rising folds, that towered
> Fold above fold a surging maze, his head
> Crested aloft, and carbuncle his eyes;
> With burnished neck of verdant gold, erect
> Amidst his circling spires, that on the grass
> Floated redundant: pleasing was his shape,
> And lovely, never since of serpent kind
> Lovelier, not those that in Illyria changed
> Hermione and Cadmus, or the god
> In Epidaurus; nor to which transformed
> Ammonian Jove, or Capitoline was seen,
> He with Olympias, this with her who bore
> Scipio the height of Rome. With tract oblique
> At first, as one who sought access, but feared
> To interrupt, sidelong he works his way.

(IX.494–512)

Milton was not a writer to give much credence to mystical texts, of which the Jewish kabbalah was a kind. But in *Paradise Lost* he created a Puritan, republican kabbalah, in which Satan is balanced with the Son as a key character. It is no surprise with these revelations concerning the poetry to find elsewhere in Milton's writing no engagement in the process of conversion, no extensive registering of repentance—in short, no high noon with Saint Augustine.[3] No more can Satan repent (IV.93–97). Rather, in so many ways, Milton wants to be the Son. He is Satan. He is Samson. There is no bridge that cancels the deficit.

If *Paradise Lost* is a new Bible, *Samson Agonistes* is a new Old Testament. It is a poem where the most painful personal and public realities are focused claustrophobically inside one figure, and where English strophes like steel cable mythologize slavery on all these levels at once:

> O glorious strength
> Put to the labour of a beast, debased
> Lower then bond-slave! Promise was that I
> Should Israel from Philistian yoke deliver;
> Ask for this great deliverer now, and find him
> Eyeless in Gaza at the mill with slaves,
> Himself in bonds under Philistian yoke;
> Yet stay, let me not rashly call in doubt
> Divine prediction; what if all foretold

> Had been fulfilled but through mine own default,
> Whom have I to complain of but myself?
>
> (lines 36–46)

Satan's speech at the start of *Paradise Lost,* Book IV, may have begun life as a soliloquy in a projected tragedy, but Samson's austerity makes Satan look interestingly reflective in his anguish by comparison:

> Then had I not been thus exiled from light;
> As in the land of darkness yet in light,
> To live a life half dead, a living death,
> And buried; but O yet more miserable!
> My self, my sepulchre, a moving grave,
> Buried, yet not exempt
> By privilege of death and burial
> From worst of other evils, pains and wrongs,
> But made hereby obnoxious more
> To all the miseries of life,
> Life in captivity
> Among inhuman foes.
>
> (lines 98–109)

Sensory deprivation and incarceration incur a grim awareness in Samson and the reader that he is on the verge of psychological depravation or even regression. It is a grim place, alleviated only by our awareness that some of this suffering is self-inflicted and could be worsened only by the appearance of a torturer. The verse seems to leave behind the sense of regular lines on the page to become bare, irreducible units of sense in space, a description of heroic identity where the gap between words and things has disappeared:

> Can this be he,
>
> That heroic, that renowned,
> Irresistible Samson? whom unarmed
> No strength of man, or fiercest wild beast could withstand;
> Who tore the lion, as the lion tears the kid,
> Ran on embattled armies clad in iron,
> And weaponless himself,
> Made arms ridiculous, useless the forgery
> Of brazen shield and spear, the hammered cuirass,
> Chalybean-tempered steel, and frock of mail
> Adamantean proof.

(lines 124–134)

The final list of armored garb, which we might imagine crumpling under Samson's blows, is a further reduction, a list without conjunctions like a line of warriors, where the final "Adamantean proof" is a reversal of normal usage, since "proof" is half the name for impenetrable plate armor ("proof armour") and "adamantean" the only instance in the *Oxford English Dictionary* of an adjectival usage referring to the hardest of substances. Riddlelike, it is not "proof" against Samson's might, and no "proof" of anything. Samson himself lives in a world in which he knows that God guides him as his chosen one, but he has lost his inner sense of God's presence and has incurred God's displeasure even while what he feels to be mere contingencies (the perfidy of his first wife, for instance) stand in his way.

The strict adherence to the timescape of the Book of Judges coupled with obviously contemporary frames of reference produce a sense of allegory buried deep within Samson's agony: an allegory of a people and all people. The chorus talks directly about atheism, and a God who appears unjust and contradictory, but it is Samson and Samson's exchanges with his antagonists that reveal a painful entity real beyond mere rational language:

> My griefs not only pain me
> As a lingering disease,
> But finding no redress, ferment and rage,
> Nor less then wounds immedicable
> Rankle, and fester, and gangrene,
> To black mortification.
> Thoughts my tormenters armed with deadly stings
> Mangle my apprehensive tenderest parts,
> Exasperate, exulcerate, and raise
> Dire inflammation which no cooling herb
> Or med'cinal liquor can assuage,

Nor breath of vernal air from snowy Alp.
Sleep hath forsook and given me o'er
To deaths benumbing opium as my only cure.
Thence faintings, swoonings of despair,
And sense of heav'n's desertion.

(lines 617–632)

The drama is one colossal writhe against tyranny and slavery. There's a lot about reason and the lapses of reason in it, but essentially it is about the spirit and the spirit of a people coming to terms with a higher reason with which they can never quite commune (or where the certainty of communication is only remembered). The casting off of bondage involves violence and, in the drama, violent language; hence the moral qualms that the work has excited. These are risks that Samson himself knows.

Thus Milton's achievement in *Samson Agonistes* has been seen as appealing directly to national crises, but in majestically unforgettable dramatic poetry:

Milton matters, then, because with Samson Agonistes we see America, along with England, "responding to its tragedy," as Derek Walcott urges it to do, "with tragic poetry" that makes a nation's eyes "clear with grief." Milton matters because, in facing tragedy, he forces us to reach beyond an axis of good and evil in the world to a more ambiguous reality . . . In *Samson Agonistes,* Milton creates a tragedy that in its aftermath resonates with history—a poem in which there seems to be a causal relationship between personal tragedy and national disaster, between Samson defeated and a nation in ruins, and in which Milton not only stages the crises of his culture but structures a critique of them . . . in his last poems, Milton casts his lot with those who worked not for the undoing of the human race but for its betterment and who, planting good where others had sown evil, would still build a new world on the wreckage of failed dreams. This last point, Milton's final poems—all of them—speak in a chorus. Samson Agonistes makes it in thunder.[4]

III

This astonishing literature does not seem to lend itself to coherence. Its aesthetic accomplishment means in part that logical completion is sought in vain. And yet so many Milton critics have argued for such a consistency—or at least they have since Milton's reputation recovered from the beating he took at the hands of the modernists in the early twentieth century. It was necessary for C. S. Lewis to defend Milton as a great Christian poet while missing that he was a great nonconformist and republican Christian poet, even a heretical poet. Stanley Fish has always pursued the case of a "right side up" Milton, a poet who played with the devil in order to show us right-minded readers the ways of sin, and has held that Milton was always fundamentally a theological writer. No less compelling and no less right are those who see Milton as irremediably of the devil's party. There is a kind of attractiveness in the perversion of this position, in its sustained attempt to make a forensic argument for that which will never quite stick.

Inviting difference and dissent is precisely what Milton's writings do, so to that extent this kind of criticism is anticipated in his work. The fact is that Milton is both theistic and post-theistic, monotheistic and polyglot—all of these positions at once. For many, this is precisely the condition of our modernity. We can see things through satanic eyes and be inspired by the Holy Spirit.

Fish's insistence that the permissive voice of God always prevails over a plurality of voices and "the face of difference" does not finally convince me: the energy of difference in Milton is too great, and Fish is in this instance such a long way away from Milton's text.[5] To claim that Milton always looked to an inspiration and a destiny not of this world is not to say, as Fish does, that Milton did not believe in action in this world. That is a recipe for boring reading, and it is untrue. The more exciting and truer insight is that all Milton's writing points to the fact that there are such possibilities—that, for better or for worse, we are urged to act. Fish berates those who treat Milton as a political prophet, one who is almost always appropriated by liberal left-wingers. Not without justification in some instances, he argues that Milton would have taken a right-wing position if alive today. He would have supported, alleges Fish, the invasion of Iraq. But more important, Fish thinks it is no business of literary critics to make political pronouncements, even if they are embodied in Milton's poetry.[6] But how can this be avoided? How can aesthetics and politics be so readily dissociated? Such a coalescence makes Milton more remarkable as a poet, not less.

Barbara Lewalski puts the matter neatly:

In an era rife with efforts to restrict the free exchange of ideas—whether by harsh restrictions on speech and press in many totalitarian regimes, or fatwas against supposedly blasphemous Salman Rushdies; or, closer to home, by efforts to ban the teaching of *The Adventures of Huckleberry Finn* or of evolution in the schools, or efforts to block some speakers on university campuses, or government manipulation of news about the necessity for and costs of the war against Iraq, or efforts to demonize dissent in times of crisis as unpatriotic—we need the stirring testimony of *Areopagitica* to the vital importance of the free flow of ideas. We need to be reminded in Milton's graphic metaphor of the overarching wrong done by suppressing books and the ideas they contain, despite the danger some may find in them.[7]

But, she goes on, Milton himself had a way of connecting the aesthetic and the poetic with the ethical and the political:

Even more important for Milton's modern readers are the poetic worlds created by his major poems. Milton meant the imaginative experiences those poems offer to be educative, supposing that they could help produce discerning, virtuous, liberty-loving human beings and citizens. Great literary works wed highly significant content to a just and appropriate form. Milton's major poems portray in magnificent verse the intellectual and moral complexities of human life, engaging both characters and readers in the hard tasks of knowing and choosing amid such complexities . . . We can determine Milton's position on some of these questions, but, as there is no narrative or interpretative voice in this drama, it offers no ready and easy answers to any of them. Rather, it forces a profound engagement with them through the experience of the characters and the resonances of the deeply moving poetic language.[8]

It is these kinds of views that, as it happens, have encouraged scholars from various disciplines (literature, history, philosophy, theology) to reconsider the relationship between Milton's writings and the history of Western thought. It has been possible to see with renewed accuracy how in the later seventeenth century Milton was considered a truly heretical writer, a fellow traveler of the deists, who alleged that God could be known simply from nature without any specific revelation.[9] Could the great Dutch Jewish theorist of matter and of toleration, Baruch Spinoza, have read *Areopagitica?* Eighteenth-century Germans certainly read Milton with a passion, resulting in a crucial encounter between the text of *Paradise Lost* and Kant. His important philosophy of perception is now seen to be profoundly indebted to Milton, something that was hitherto unnoticed: not just to Milton's thought but to the nature of his poetry too.[10] There are certainly dangers that would lead to a forgetting of Milton in a world of dry Milton scholarship, but critical, historically informed investigations need to take place if stereotypical views of Milton—for instance, as the father of American liberalism—are to be tested or resisted.

Yet the degree to which key Miltonic themes have penetrated popular culture, including a substantial impact on cinema, but also on science fiction novels, visual texts, rock songs, and children's literature, is a measure of the enduring appeal of the key characters, especially Satan, as well as of the epic; so too the subject of teaching Milton itself.[11] Woody Allen characters played by Woody Allen have conversations in hell with the devil about Milton. In films, profligate professors from thinly disguised but well-known liberal arts colleges teach Milton very badly before sleeping with their students. James T. Kirk of the starship *Enterprise* read Milton; so did his enemies. If Milton was seen by some in the debates concerning the literary canon of the past twenty-five years as a conservative figure, that was a measure of academic co-optation and standing. Popular culture tells a very different story.

Philosophy, then, as much as poetry, has become truly Miltonic, and perhaps it is the plotting, characterization, and language of poets, novelists, and playwrights that made and makes Milton's influence so pervasive and extensive. This is so even to the extent of a re-reading of Milton's works and in particular of *Paradise Lost* for the sake of a radical reappraisal of the nature of the verse itself. In this new aesthetic view, Miltonic blank verse is an even more responsive, fluid, and fast-moving tool than we thought. To prove this view, some old assumptions, such as the acceptance of the original printed punctuation of the poem, has gone by the board. Such an approach has not won easy approval, although it has given new life to the appreciation of the poem, and it is this, in the context of the acknowledged split vision between monotheism, polytheism, and mantheism, that is valuable.[12] We are beginning to understand Milton's "over-going," rebellious theology, his social theory, and its impact on our culture, but we still have a way to go. What does seem never-ending is the capacity of Milton's verse to engender these forces of ardent protest and ethical activism, even as that verse is so magnificent and visionary in its construction. Take the verse, read it, and start to think your liberty through again even as the poetry ennobles.

NOTES

SELECT BIBLIOGRAPHY

INDEX

NOTES

Introduction

1. See Annabel Patterson, *Early Modern Liberalism* (Cambridge University Press, 1997), ch. 8; Keith W. F. Stavely, *Puritan Legacies: Paradise Lost and the New England Tradition, 1630–1890* (Cornell University Press, 1987); Lydia Dittler Schulman, *Paradise Lost and the Rise of the American Republic* (Northeastern University Press, 1992), K. P. Van Anglen, *The New England Milton: Literary Reception and Cultural Authority in the Early Republic* (Pennsylvania State University Press, 1993). For a consideration of *Paradise Lost* in the context of moral and pastoral counsel, see Margaret Oluf Thickstun, *Milton's Paradise Lost: Moral Education* (New York: Palgrave Macmillan, 2007). My discussion is also influenced by Paul Bové's forthcoming work on the place of Milton in the American academy, and by Lindsay Waters, "Poetry. Well-educated. Pity," *Providence* (Summer 1998): 32–42.

2. Thomas N. Corns, "Milton's Quest for Respectability," in J. Martin Evans, ed.,

John Milton: Twentieth-Century Perspectives, vol. 1, *The Man and the Author* (Routledge, 2003), 219–229.

3. See Ken Hiltner, *Milton and Ecology* (Cambridge University Press, 2003).

1. Poetics and Poetic Strategies

1. Even if *Samson Agonistes* was originally written at an earlier stage: see *CSP,* 349–350.

2. See the dispute engendered by John Carey, "A Work in Praise of Terrorism? September 11 and *Samson Agonistes," Times Literary Supplement,* 6 Sept. 2002, 15.

2. Divorce

1. B. J. Sokol, "'Tilted Lees,' Dragons, Haemony, Menarche, Spirit, and Matter in *Comus," Review of English Studies* n.s. 41 (1990), 349–324.

2. Plato, *Symposium,* 203; Gen. 2:18–24. See also the reference to the story of Eros and Anteros (Plato, *Phaedrus,* 255d), *The Doctrine and Discipline of Divorce, CPW,* II.254–256.

3. As in the case of the 1630s Colchester sectaries John Farnham and Richard Bull and their followers: see Naomi Baker, ed., *Scripture Women: Rose Thurgood, 'A Lecture of Repentance' and Cicely Jonson, 'Fanatical Reveries'* (Nottingham Trent University Press, 2005), xiv–xvii.

4. See Richard Overton, *Mans Mortalitie (1643),* ed. Harold Fisch (Liverpool: Liverpool University Press, 1968), p. 10; Milton, *The Doctrine and Discipline of Divorce, CPW,* III.373. I am grateful to Kate Thomas for this insight.

3. Free Will

1. Hesiod, *Theogony,* 570 ff.

2. Homer, *Iliad,* I, 1; *Odyssey,* I, 9, 32; Manilius, *Astronomicon,* IV, 108–118.

4. Tyranny and Kingship

1. Martin Dzelzainis, "Milton, Macbeth, and Buchanan," *Seventeenth Century* 4 (1989): 53–66.

2. The abbreviation MDz. here and below stands for John Milton, *Political Writings,* ed. Martin Dzelzainis (Cambridge: Cambridge University Press, 1991).

3. See Neil Forsyth, *The Satanic Epic* (Princeton University Press, 2003).

5. Free States

1. James Hankins, "'Res publica' in the Italian Renaissance," unpublished paper presented at the Renaissance Studies Colloquium, Princeton University, Princeton, N.J., 10 November 2005. For an argument that it was the encounter with Hebraic republicanism that produced the view that republicanism was the only proper constitution, see Eric Nelson, "'Talmudical Commonwealthsmen' and the Rise of Republican Exclusivism," *Historical Journal* 50 (2007): 837–859.

6. Imagining Creation

1. John Rogers, "Milton and the Heretical Priesthood of Christ," in D. Loewenstein and J. Marshall, eds., *Heresy, Literature, and Politics in Early Modern English Culture* (Cambridge University Press, 2006), 203–220.

2. See Andrew Marvell, *The First Anniversary of the Government under His Highness the Lord Protector* (1654–1655), in Andrew Marvell, *Poems,* ed. Nigel Smith (Longman, 2003), 281–298, lines 45–84.

3. I am indebted here to the ongoing work of Joanna Picciotto on Milton and the new science. See Joanna Picciotto, "Reforming the Garden: The Experimentalist Eden and *Paradise Lost,*" *Journal of English Literary History* 72 (2005): 23–78.

4. Letters from John Beale to John Evelyn, November 1667–February 1671; Evelyn Collection, MS 15948 ff. 136, 138, British Library, London.

7. The Lover, the Poem, and the Critics

1. Norberto Bobbio and Maurizio Viroli, *The Idea of the Republic*, trans. Allan Cameron (Polity, 2003); John P. McCormick, "Machiavelli Against Republicanism: On the Cambridge School's 'Guicciardinian Moments,'" *Political Theory* 31, 5 (2003): 615–643.

2. John Milton, *Paradise* Lost, ed. with introduction by Philip Pullman (Oxford University Press, 2005), as quoted on Amazon.com.

3. Stephen M. Fallon, *Milton's Peculiar Grace: Self-Representation and Authority* (Cornell University Press, 2007), ix–x.

4. Joseph Wittreich, "Why Milton Matters," *Milton Studies* 44 (2005): 22–39.

5. Stanley Fish, *How Milton Works* (Harvard University Press, 2001), 567.

6. Stanley Fish, "Why Milton Matters; Or, Against Historicism," *Milton Studies* 44 (2005): 11.

7. "Barbara Lewalski on Why Milton Matters," *Milton Studies* 44 (2005): 14.

8. Ibid., 16.

9. Abraham Stoll, "Discontinuous Wound: Milton and Deism," *Milton Studies* 44 (2005): 179–202.

10. Sanford Budick, "Kant's Miltonic Test of Talent: The Presence of 'When I Consider' in the Groundwork of the Metaphysics of Morals," *Modern Language Quarterly* 61 (2000): 481–518.

11. Laura Lunger Knoppers and Gregory M. Colón Semenza, eds., *Milton in Popular Culture* (Palgrave Macmillan, 2006).

12. Gordon Teskey, *Delirious Milton* (Harvard University Press, 2006).

SELECT BIBLIOGRAPHY

The number of editions of Milton's writings and of books and articles concerned with the man, his times, and his works is vast. What follows is a list of available texts and critical studies that provide helpful insights, including several that are considered influential or essential reading. Space limitations prevent me from mentioning many worthy studies. The works below contain more detailed bibliographies, especially in the "companion" section.

Editions of Milton's Writings

There are many different editions of Milton's poetry, especially of *Paradise Lost,* many with much useful information in introductions, headnotes, and footnotes. The debate over whether or not to modernize Milton's text is intense and unlikely to be resolved quickly.

Poetry

Carey, John, ed. *Complete Shorter Poems,* 2d ed. Longman, 1997.

Fowler, Alastair, ed. *Paradise Lost,* 2d ed. Longman, 1998.

Kastan, David Scott, ed. *Paradise Lost.* Hackett, 2005.

Leonard, John, ed. *The Complete Poems.* Penguin, 1998.

———, ed. *Paradise Lost.* Penguin, 2003.

Leonard, John, and Christopher Ricks. *Selected Poems.* Penguin, 2007.

Ricks, Christopher, ed. *Paradise Lost and Paradise Regained.* Signet Classics, 2001.

Prose

Dzelzainis, Martin, ed. *Political Writings.* Cambridge University Press, 1991. Very helpful notes.

Patrides, C. A., ed. *John Milton: Selected Prose.* Penguin, 1974; rev. ed. University of Missouri Press, 1985. The most useful single volume of the prose.

Wolfe, Don M., ed. *Complete Prose Works of John Milton.* 8 vols. Yale University Press, 1953–1983. The standard modern edition.

Poetry and Prose

Campbell, Gordon, ed. *Complete English Poems; Of Education; Areopagitica.* Everyman, 1980 et seq.

Flannagan, Roy, ed. *The Riverside Milton.* Houghton Mifflin, 1998.

Hughes, Merritt Y., ed. *Complete Poems and Major Prose.* Hackett, 2003.

Kerrigan, William, Stephen M. Fallon, and John P. Rumrich, eds. *Complete Poetry and Essential Prose.* Random House, 2007.

Pullman, Philip, ed. *Paradise Lost.* Oxford University Press, 2005.

Website

The Milton Reading Room, www.dartmouth.edu/~milton. Run by Thomas
Luxon, of Dartmouth College, this is a great resource. In addition to texts
of the major works, it has a comprehensive bibliography of recent criticism.

Biography

Hill, Christopher. *Milton and the English Revolution.* Faber and Faber, 1977.

Lewalski, Barbara. *The Life of John Milton.* Blackwell, 2000.

Parker, W. R. *Milton. A Biography.* 2 vols. Oxford University Press, 1968. The
classic account of Milton as a Renaissance humanist in the continental
arena. Supplemented with W. R. Parker, *Milton: A Biographical Commentary,* ed. Gordon Campbell (Oxford: Oxford University Press, 1996).

Companions

Corns, Thomas N., ed. *A Companion to Milton.* Blackwell Companions to
Literature and Culture. Blackwell, 2001.

Danielson, Dennis, ed. *The Cambridge Companion to Milton.* Rev. ed. Cambridge University Press, 1999.

Criticism

General Works

Achinstein, Sharon. *Literature and Dissent in Milton's England.* Cambridge
University Press, 2004.

Bennett, Joan. *Reviving Liberty: Radical Christian Humanism in Milton's
Great Poems.* Harvard University Press, 1989.

Christopher, Georgia B. *Milton and the Science of the Saints.* Princeton University Press, 1982.

Corns, Thomas N. *Milton's Language.* Blackwell, 1990.

Danielson, Dennis. *Milton's Good God: A Study in Literary Theodicy.* Cambridge University Press, 1982.

Edwards, Karen L. *Milton and the Natural World: Science and Poetry in Paradise Lost.* Cambridge University Press, 1999.

Fallon, Stephen M. *Milton among the Philosophers: Poetry and Materialism in Seventeenth-Century England.* Cornell University Press, 1991.

——— *Milton's Peculiar Grace: Self-Representation and Authority.* Cornell University Press, 2007.

Fish, Stanley. *How Milton Works.* Harvard University Press, 2001.

Herman, Peter C. *Destabilizing Milton: "Paradise Lost" and the Poetics of Incertitude* (New York: Palgrave Macmillan, 2005).

Knoppers, Laura Lunger, and Gregory M. Colón Semenza, eds. *Milton in Popular Culture.* New York, 2006.

Loewenstein, David. *Milton and the Drama of History: Historical Vision, Iconoclasm, and the Literary Imagination.* Cambridge University Press, 1990.

——— *Representing Revolution in Milton and His Contemporaries.* Cambridge University Press, 2001.

Parry, Graham, and Joad Raymond, eds. *Milton and the Terms of Liberty.* D. S. Brewer, 2002.

Patterson, Annabel. *Reading between the Lines.* University of Wisconsin Press, 1993. Includes chapters on Milton.

———, ed. *John Milton.* Longman Critical Reader. Longman, 1992.

Rogers, John. *The Matter of Revolution. Science, Poetry and Politics in the Age of Milton.* Cornell University Press, 1996.

Rosenblatt, Jason. *Torah and Law in Paradise Lost.* Princeton University Press, 1994.

Teskey, Gordon. *Delirious Milton.* Harvard University Press, 2005.

Turner, James Grantham. *One Flesh. Paradisal Marriage and Sexual Relations in the Age of Milton.* Oxford University Press, 1987.

Early Poetry

Brown, Cedric. *John Milton's Aristocratic Entertainments.* Cambridge University Press, 1984.

Evans, J. Martin. *The Miltonic Moment.* University Press of Kentucky, 1998.

Guillory, John. *Spenser, Milton and Literary History.* Columbia University Press, 1983.

Hollander, John. *The Figure of Echo: A Mode of Allusion in Milton and After.* University of California Press, 1981.

Norbrook, David. *Poetry and Politics in the English Renaissance.* Rev. ed. Oxford University Press, 2002. Chap. 10.

Prince, F. T. *The Italian Element in Milton's Verse.* Oxford University Press, 1954.

Revard, Stella P. *Milton and the Tangles of Neaera's Hair: The Making of the 1645 Poems.* University of Missouri Press, 1997.

Paradise Lost

Burrow, Colin. *Epic Romance: Homer to Milton.* Oxford University Press, 1993.

Empson, William. *Milton's God.* Rev. ed. Cambridge University Press, 1981.

Fish, Stanley. *Surprised by Sin: The Reader in Paradise Lost.* 2d ed. Harvard University Press, 1998.

Leonard, John. *Naming in Paradise: Milton and the Language of Adam and Eve.* Oxford University Press, 1990.

Lewalski, Barbara K. *Paradise Lost and the Rhetoric of Literary Forms.* Princeton University Press, 1985.

Lewis, C. S. *A Preface to Paradise Lost.* Oxford University Press, 1960.

Poole, William. *Milton and the Idea of the Fall.* Cambridge University Press, 2005.

Quint, David. *Epic and Empire: Politics and Generic Form from Virgil to Milton.* Princeton University Press, 1993.

Ricks, Christopher. *Milton's Grand Style.* Oxford University Press, 1963.

Rumrich, John P. *Matter of Glory: A New Preface to Paradise Lost.* University of Pittsburgh Press, 1987.

Schwartz, Regina M. *Remembering and Repeating: Biblical Creation in Paradise Lost.* Cambridge University Press, 1988.

Paradise Regained and *Samson Agonistes*

Knoppers, Laura Lunger. *Historicizing Milton: Spectacle, Power, and Poetry in Restoration England.* University of Georgia Press, 1994.

Lewalski, Barbara K. *Milton's Brief Epic: The Genre, Meaning, and Art of* Paradise Regained. Brown University Press, 1966.

Radzinowicz, Mary Ann. *Towards* Samson Agonistes: *The Growth of Milton's Mind.* Princeton University Press, 1978.

Wittreich, Joseph. *Shifting Contexts: Reinterpreting Samson Agonistes.* Duquesne University Press, 2002.

Prose

Armitage, David, et al., eds. *Milton and Republicanism.* Cambridge University Press, 1995.

Corns, Thomas N. *Uncloistered Virtue: English Political Literature.* Oxford University Press, 1992.

Cable, Lana. *Carnal Knowledge: Milton's Iconoclasm and the Poetics of Desire.* Duke University Press, 1995.

Hoxby, Blair. *Mammon's Music: Literature and Economics in the Age of Milton.* Yale University Press, 2002.

Kahn, Victoria. *Wayward Contracts: The Crisis of Political Obligation in England, 1640–1674.* Princeton University Press, 2004.

Loewenstein, David, and James Grantham Turner, eds. *Politics, Poetics and Hermeneutics in Milton's Prose.* Cambridge University Press, 1990.

Norbrook, David. *Writing the English Republic: Poetry, Rhetoric and Politics 1627–1660.* Cambridge University Press, 1999.

Smith, Nigel. *Literature and Revolution in England 1640–1660.* Yale University Press, 1994.

Von Maltzahn, Nicholas. *Milton's History of Britain: Republican Historiography in the English Revolution.* Oxford University Press, 1991.

Journals

There are two journals devoted to Milton: *Milton Studies* and *Milton Quarterly.* Both are also available upon subscription as e-journals. *Milton Quarterly* can be found at http://www.blackwellpublishing .com/journal.asp?ref= 0026-4326&site=1. *Milton Studies* is published annually by the University of Pittsburgh Press and can be found at http://www.upress.pitt.edu.

INDEX

Calvinists, 130

Canon law, 52

Canzone, 18

Cape of Good Hope, 127

Caracalla, Antoninus, 96

Carey, John, 156

Caribbean Sea, 127

Cathaian coast, 146

Catharsis, 63

Cave of Mammon, 71

Ceres, 115, 170

Cham (Ammon), 170

Chaos, 11–12, 26–27, 60, 104, 127, 145–148

Chapman, George, 19

Charity, 47

Charles I (king of England), 10, 59, 87, 90, 92–93, 100, 119, 124; *Eikon Basilike,* 31, 91–92

Charles II (king of England), 98, 119

Charybdis, 147

Chases, 53

Chastity, 21, 45

Chaucer, Geoffrey, 20

Choice, 68, 72–73

Christ. *See* Son, the

Christ's College, Cambridge, 7

Christian fundamentalism, 2

Church, Christian, 69

Church, primitive Christian, 53

Church architecture, 35

Church of England, 22, 26; Act of Conformity (1662), 129

Cicero, Marcus Tullius, 25, 110

Cincinnatus, Lucius Quintius, 120

Citizenship, 110

City-states, ancient, 29

Civic duty, 39

Civil War, English, 8

Cleaving, 50

Cleopatra, 40, 94

Coition, 43–44, 56, 158, 173

Cold war, 3

Colossians 2:17, 171

Columbus, Christopher, 127

Comedy, Restoration, 94

Commodities, 75

Commonwealth, Christian, 30–31

Communication, 3, 73

Communion, 83

Communism, 3

Complaint, 22

Comus, 28, 45, 49

Conceit, poetic, 15

Confusion, 26, 51

Constitutional reform, 87

Contradiction, 7, 10–12, 89

Contrariness/contrariety, 7–8, 28, 50, 73

Conversation, 46

God *(continued)*
101–102, 104, 127, 174; God's
love, 162–163; God's wrath, 85
Graces, Three, 169
Grammar, 104
Greece, 29, 118
Greek language, 19
Grotius, Hugo, 52
Guilds, 75
Guyon, 71

Hagar, 130
Hair, 42, 57
Hall, John, of Durham, 116–117
Hamburg, 115
Hamlet, 12
Harapha, 38, 94
Harrington, James, 5, 118
Hatred, 50
Heaven, 17, 97, 101, 123, 162
Hebrew language, 19
Hebrews (Bible): Heb. 9:24, 137;
Heb. 12:2, 135
Hell, 24, 97–98, 101, 123, 146, 161;
Gates of, 27
Herbert, George, 15
Hercules, 90, 114
Heresy, 7, 9, 13, 69, 134, 184
Hermes, 172
Hermetic tradition, 150

Hermione, 185
Hesiod, 173
Hierarchy, 103
Historical writing, 110
History plays, 97
Hobbes, Thomas, 5, 36, 125; *Leviathan,* 36
Homer, 69
Homeric Hymn to Demeter, 170
Horace, 112, 116
Horatian Ode, An (Marvell), 116
Horticulture, 63
Hotspur, 40
House of Lords, 110
Hydrodynamics, 151

Icon Animorum (Barclay), 27
Ideas, 74
Idolatry, 51, 85, 89, 92, 99
Image, 36; image of God, 136–137, 139–140
Imperialism, 2–3, 97, 120, 127, 131
Incest, 32, 95–96
Incompatibility, 48
Ind (India), 97
Independents (Congregationalists), 80
Indian Ocean, 127
Infanticide, 95

Lewalski, Barbara, 183–184
Lewis, C. S., 181
Liberalism, 1–2, 185
Libertinism, 9
Liberty, 2, 4–5, 11, 97, 103, 110, 114, 119, 124, 129, 131, 186
Liberty Fund, 4
Licensing of books, 9–10, 73–76, 98–99, 116
Livy (Titus Livius), 126
Logic, 104
London, 70, 87; Bread Street, 86; Holborn, 86; Lincoln's Inn Fields, 86; St. Paul's School, 7
Longinus, Dionysius, 116
Love, 50, 155–173
Lucan, Marcus Annaeus, 116–117; *De bello civili,* 122
Luscinus, Gaius Fabricius, 120
Lust, 56
Lutherans, 130
Luxury, 106

Macbeth (Shakespeare), 93–94
Machiavelli, Niccolò, 87, 113, 131; *Discorsi,* 126, 160
Madrigal, 17
Magistrates, 111
Mammon, 103
Manilius, Marcus, 69

Manoa, 38, 94, 160
Man's Mortalitie (Overton), 51–52
Marlowe, Christopher, 11
Marriage, 9, 45–49, 159; paradisal marriage, 43, 141
Martyrs, 25
Marvell, Andrew, 143
Masque, 92
Matthew 6:9, 130
Measure for Measure (Shakespeare), 45
Melancholy, 42
Memory, 80; art of, 29
Menstruation, 42, 52
Mercurius Politicus, 116, 126
Metamorphoses (Ovid), 170
Metaphysical Poets (Gardner), 15
Meter, 17
Microscope, 122
Middle East, 14
Militarism, 69–70
Millenarians, 103, 106
Milton, John (father), 86
Milton, John, works of:
    Paradise Lost, 5–6, 11, 15, 21–24, 27, 33–37, 40, 43, 45, 53, 65–68, 76–85, 92, 96–99, 101–105, 108, 119–127, 129, 132–154, 157–158, 161–165, 177, 184, 186
    Paradise Regained, 6, 11, 36–38,

Peter, Saint, 22, 148

Petrarch (Francesco Petrarca), 18, 30, 112, 116, 155

Philistines, 38, 40, 58, 74, 94, 99, 107, 159–160, 176

Phillips, Edward, 86

Piedmont, 113

Platonic philosophy, 48–49

Poet, role of the, 29–30

Poetry, art of, 5, 29

Political theory, 110

Polonius, 40, 94

Polygamy, 53

Pompey (Gnaeus Pompeius Magnus), 122

Popular culture, 185

Popularity, 123, 161

Portugal, 127

Powell, Mary (Milton's first wife), 86, 109

Prayer, 92, 138

Presbyterians, 27, 51, 76, 81, 87–89, 93, 112, 120

Press freedom, 4, 9, 109

Priapus, 100

Priesthood, 7

Print, 73

Proairesis (choice), 68–69

Prometheus, 173

Promiscuity, 45

Prophecy, 17–18, 21–22

Proserpine, 169–171

Protectorate, Cromwellian, 6, 112, 127

Protestantism, 25

Psyche, 72

Ptolemy (Claudius Ptolomaeus), 149

Public sphere, 70–71

Pullman, Philip, 12, 166–167

Purgatorio (Dante), 160

Puritans, 2, 8, 10, 37–38, 53–54, 80–81, 129–29, 131, 176

Pyramids, 99

Quintius (Lucius Quinctius Cincinnatus), 106

Radicalism, religious, 9, 80–81

Rape, 53, 58

Reading, 27–28, 72

Reason, 36–37, 58, 65, 70–71, 77–79, 96

Rebellion, 7, 10, 77, 98, 103

Reformation, Protestant, 29

Regicide, 11, 95, 110

Regulus, Marcus Atilius, 106, 120

Repetition, 36

Reproduction, 44–46, 48, 58, 63

Republicanism, 2, 5–6, 37, 75, 87, 97, 108–126, 160, 176; classical, 89